Benny Go

Already published volumes in the
JAZZ MASTERS SERIES

JAZZ MASTERS SERIES

Benny Goodman

BRUCE CROWTHER

Discography by
Bruce Crowther

First published in Great Britain in 1988 by
APOLLO PRESS LIMITED
11 Baptist Gardens, London NW5 4ET

© Bruce Crowther 1988

British Library Cataloguing in Publication Data
Crowther, Bruce
    Benny Goodman.—(Jazz masters series; 13)
    1. Goodman, Benny   2. Jazz musicians—
    United States—Biography
    I. Title   II. Series
    785.42'092'4   ML410.G6/

ISBN 0-948820-04-7

Series editor: David Burnett James

Typesetting by concept Crayford, Kent

Printed and Bound in Great Britain by
Anchor Brendon Limited, Tiptree, Essex

Contents

Illustrations

Preface

To become a legend before the age of thirty is a distinction granted to few men; to remain a legend for the next half-century requires extraordinary qualities.

Not long after his twenty-fifth birthday Benny Goodman was a national celebrity, a figure of international repute, and a millionaire; in 1984 he celebrated his seventy-fifth birthday and was still going strong. He was more than ever capable of packing a concert hall anywhere in the world for both jazz and classical concerts, and was even richer. His death in 1986 finally ended an era of music more than half a century after its inception.

During his career he graduated from child prodigy to King of Swing to renowned classicist, and along the way established a reputation as a hard-headed businessman with a contrary streak of eccentricity.

Somewhere amidst the legend, the public acclaim, the best-selling records, the fortune, and the music-making, lies the real man and the real Benny Goodman story.   B.C.

Acknowledgements

I am most grateful to a number of people who have offered advice, loaned me records and allowed me to hear interviews they have taped with musicians and, in some instances, just talked while I listened: Bill Berry, Roger Dalleywater, Val Ebenezersson, Andrew Gardner, Geoff Organ, Nat Pierce and Mike Pinfold.

Chapter One

In many respects Benny Goodman's story resembles a Horatio Alger novel: poor boy from an immigrant family rises to fame and fortune through hard work, innate talent and steely determination. It is the American Dream personified, the kind of story Hollywood loves although, needless to say, when a movie was made about Benny it contrived to be both untruthful and to trivialise his achievements.

Benny's mother and father came to America separately in the 1890s. He was from Warsaw, she from Kovno, both were Jews and suffered as did so many under the tyranny of Czarist domination. David Goodman met Dora in Baltimore where they married and began raising what would eventually be a very large family. By 1903, when they moved to Chicago, they already had three children and later they would add nine more although one did not grow to adulthood. The ninth-born child was named Benjamin David and whatever hopes the family had for him they cannot have imagined how much he would actually accomplish.

Benny was born on 30 May, 1909 in a house on Francisco Avenue located on Chicago's West side. His father worked in a clothing factory where the hours were long and the work arduous. Benny would later recall that his father rarely earned more than $20 a week and that sometimes the family had, literally, nothing to eat. He also recalled that David Goodman, Pop, enjoyed music and would take his family to Sunday afternoon band concerts in Douglas Park.

When Pop Goodman learned that free music lessons were available at the Kehelah Jacob Synagogue, just a mile and a half from

9

home, he enrolled three of his sons there and when this tuition folded somehow managed to raise enough money to allow them to continue their studies at Jane Addams' famous settlement house. At Hull-House the three Goodman boys improved rapidly: Harry played trombone, then switched to tuba, Freddy learned trumpet, while Benny, the youngest and smallest of the trio, was allocated the clarinet. The instrument appealed to him right from the start, although at first it was the shiny keys that held most attraction.

At Hull-House Benny was tutored by Franz Schoepp, a German-born musician who taught at Chicago's Musical College and had formerly been a player in symphony orchestras. Benny's earliest tuition on the clarinet was, therefore, orthodox and classically-based. Schoepp's pupils included Buster Bailey and even the great Jimmy Noone was not above taking lessons from the old man.

About the same time that he was attending Schoepp's classes Benny was also listening eagerly to records by the popular entertainer Ted Lewis and copied one of his tunes until he was note-perfect. Encouraged by the eldest of his brothers, Louis, Benny entered an amateur contest at the Central Park Theatre. Too young and too small to appear on-stage he had to stand in the pit. He didn't win but he impressed the theatre owner enough for him to be called in some time later as substitute for another act. This was for a daytime show and he was allowed to perform on-stage. More importantly, he was paid $5. Benny Goodman had earned his first money from playing the clarinet.

For a young kid from a poverty-wracked immigrant family $5 was a huge sum and his eyes were opened to the possibilities that lay ahead. Whatever musical ambitions lurked inside little Benny's skinny frame, there can be no doubt that the desire to lift himself and his family out of their poverty-trap was of paramount importance in shaping his future – and his attitude towards money.

For the moment, however, he could only dream of the future and enjoy the pleasure of taking money home to his hard-up parents. He was, after all, only twelve years old.

Apart from their lessons, Benny and his brother Harry also played in the Hull-House band. The band's musical director was Jimmy Sylvester who also had his own band which played dances around Chicago, often at school proms. Whether attending school, or playing school dances, or visiting other dances just to listen, Benny was soon involved either socially or professionally with cornetist Jimmy McPartland, Jimmy's banjo-playing brother Dick, saxophonist Frank Teschemacher, drummer Davey Tough and other young members of the growing Chicago school of jazz.

Benny was also listening to, and learning from, other clarinet players either on record or in person. Among those for whom he has professed admiration were Johnny Dodds, Leon Rapollo and Volly de Faut. But there were musicians around who were beginning to listen to and admire Benny himself.

Among these admirers was tenor saxophonist Bud Freeman who, many years later, would recall that if there ever was a genius it was Benny Goodman and 'at the age of twelve he could play the clarinet backwards.' Another who admired young Benny was Charlie Podolsky who offered him work at a better class of dance date. Benny was eager to accept but now he needed a union card. He also had to start wearing long pants and sometimes a tuxedo; these were provided by his sister Ethel who worked for a clothing company. By now, he was thirteen.

As Chicago grew in importance as the current jazz centre of America, Benny was able to listen to many more musicians: Louis Armstrong, Kid Ory, Freddie Keppard, Bessie Smith, Muggsy Spanier and the New Orleans Rhythm Kings.

Working nights as he was, young Benny found school something of a problem especially when it came to getting up in the morning. Practising was a problem too as the Goodmans now lived close by Mount Sinai Hospital where patients and staff were understandably ill-disposed towards listening to even his prodigious talent. These problems were solved when Benny decided to spend some of his earnings on a private school, which Davey Tough also attended, where classes did not begin until the much more civilized hour of eleven-thirty.

By now Benny Goodman's name was becoming well-known on the Chicago music scene (although not so much so that Bix Beiderbecke couldn't throw him off the stand one night, thinking the skinny kid with glasses was fooling around with other people's instruments) and when he was asked to join Jules Herbeveaux's band at Guyon's Paradise he jumped at the chance. For this he had to make a decision: he could not play four nights a week *and* attend school. Forty eight dollars for four nights was strong competition and school

11

lost. At the time there was no legal obligation to attend school beyond the age of fourteen. It was now the autumn of 1923 and as Benny had passed his fourteenth birthday in May he dropped out.

A year after his *bar mitzvah* Benny Goodman proved he was ready for man's estate and became a full-time professional musician.

Benny's stint with the Herbeveaux band lasted only until he was offered more money to join Arnold Johnson at the Green Mill Gardens. A couple of the girls in the chorus line at this job would later make their own marks in showbiz: Helen Morgan and Ruth Etting. From there Benny moved to Art Kassel's Castles in the Air band at the Midway Gardens where Elmer Schoebel was the house pianist. A friend of Kassel's was saxophonist Gil Rodin, then with the Ben Pollack band. Rodin was immediately impressed by Benny and began taking him around town to hear the great jazzmen who either made Chicago their home or were passing through on tours. Rodin duly reported back to his boss and when Pollack began laying plans to come into Chicago from California Benny was offered a job. Scarcely able to believe his good fortune, because Ben Pollack was big-time, Benny hopped a train and went West.

Pollack's band was playing in Venice, Los Angeles and Benny joined at $100 a week. Pollack soon made his move east and Benny's brother Harry joined the band after first agreeing to switch from tuba to string bass. The money the two Goodman brothers were now earning was almost unbelievable.

The family benefited enormously, of course, and although some of their siblings were married now and living away from home there was still enough money coming in to make Pop Goodman's arduous work at the clothing factory unnecessary. He was talked into giving up his job but he insisted on keeping active and his family thought he should get as much fresh air as possible after all his years in factories and sweatshops. He therefore ran a little newspaper stand which kept him outside, active and independent. Although Benny and Harry were playing in the city, the old man kept putting off attending one of their performances until he had bought a new suit appropriate for such an occasion. Pop Goodman made a point of returning home from his newsstand early enough to eat with his youngest children. One night, as he headed homewards, he was knocked down by a car and killed.

Thus, sadly, Pop Goodman, who had done so much to direct

Benny along a musical path through life, did not live to enjoy his son's astonishing success.

The Ben Pollack band, however bigtime it might be for young Benny Goodman, far from overshadowed him. Indeed, he was soon a heavily-featured soloist and his duets with drummer Pollack were greeted eagerly by the fans. Pollack later claimed that he had first heard Benny in Chicago doing his Ted Lewis impressions and was consequently alerted to his possibilities before Gil Rodin suggested he should be hired. Certainly, Benny was well-qualified to play in the Pollack band but it is equally certain that his stint there helped round out his professionalism. It was also a period when he was able to develop his own style. Until then he was playing a stylistic mixture of the best of the men he admired most. Fortunately, none of these was an inferior musician (in jazz terms Ted Lewis was a non-starter but Benny's impressions of him were for fun, not to further his development) and this, allied to his formal schooling, gave him a solid foundation upon which to build.

During 1926 Benny made his first records, with the Pollack band, and early the following year recorded under his own name with pianist Mel Stitzel and drummer Bob Conselman, thus predating by almost a decade the more famous Benny Goodman Trio. Around this time he also played his clarinet into a dictaphone so that a publisher could transcribe and print *One Hundred Jazz Breaks by Benny Goodman* which helped bring his name even further to the fore.

During 1927 the Pollack band returned to California, then came back to Chicago and made more records including one on which Benny played trumpet in addition to clarinet. At the end of the year Benny quit the band to join up with Isham Jones in Chicago. In March, 1928 Gil Rodin talked him into rejoining Pollack who was about to take his band into New York, still the showbiz Mecca despite the prominence at this time of Chicago in the jazzman's gazetteer. The band did well at first but soon fell on hard times and Benny took jobs when and where they were offered. Pollack picked up more work and Benny rejoined for an engagement at Atlantic City's Million Dollar Pier. The personnel of the band was fluid at this time but among the regulars was trombonist Glenn Miller; Benny also found himself working alongside old friends such as Jimmy McPartland and Frank Teschemacher while new people like Jack Teagarden, the Texan trombonist, opened his ears still further.

13

McPartland would later recall the hard times when Pollack's band had no work. What seemed like the entire band would move in with Benny, Gil, Glenn and banjo-player Dick Morgan who shared a suite at the Whitby Apartments in New York. They lived by going to parties; not much food but plenty to drink, even if this was in the midst of Prohibition.

At the end of 1928 Pollack secured a year-long engagement at New York's Park Central Hotel and capped this by landing the pit job for the new Jimmy McHugh-Dorothy Fields musical show, *Hello, Daddy*. Doubling these two engagements meant that for a time at least money was not a problem for Benny and the others, although maybe sleeping was.

By mid-1929, when *Hello, Daddy* closed, Benny Goodman was twenty years old and one of the most experienced and sought-after musicians around town. As this was New York, it placed him pretty close to the top of the heap. His reputation was such that he was invited to form a band to play a date under his own name even though he was still working for Pollack. Grudgingly, Pollack agreed to this but vented some spleen by firing Jimmy McPartland for coming onto the stand wearing dirty shoes. Benny read the warning signs and offered to go too.

The next five years were to be musically profitable for Benny, although not always financially so, and his reputation continued to spread thanks due in no small part to the recordings he was now making regularly.

14

Chapter Two

Benny Goodman's very first recording date appears to have taken place back in September 1926 but none of the three tracks was issued. A couple more dates with Pollack came in December and on one tune, *'Deed I Do,* Benny solos alongside a forgettable vocal by the band's leader. Another tune from the same session, *He's the Last Word,* also has a solo by the young clarinetist but suffers from substandard vocalising, this time by The Williams Sisters. One of the sisters was married to boxer Jack Dempsey, so maybe she had influence.

It was not until February of 1927 and the recordings made under his own name and accompanied only by piano and drums that the first real assessment of Benny's ability can be made. The tunes are *That's A Plenty,* not then the hackneyed old warhorse it would become, and *Clarinetitis,* a Goodman original.

Benny's playing on these tunes, while not yet of the full virtuoso standard he was to reach, is superb. His intense performance, amidst which the influences of other clarinet players can be heard, reveals an embryonic 'Goodman-style'. It is possible to understand the impact the young musician had upon his contemporaries. While virtuosity is not, of itself, a necessary requirement of jazz, when allied to a profound feeling for hot music, such as Benny displayed at this time, he obviously stood out dramatically from those around him. Unlike the brass players of the 1920s, among whom were several technically gifted performers, early jazz reed-players often left much to be desired.

In mid-1928 Benny recorded an interesting session with Pollack, McPartland, Miller, Morgan, brother Harry and tenor-saxophonist Fud Livingston. Billed as Benny Goodman's Boys, the band recorded several tracks on which dmonstrated his multi-instrumental ability playing alto and baritone saxophones and cornet in addition to clarinet. One tune was named *Room 1411* in honour of the suite at the Whitby where the temporarily homeless Pollack band had roomed with Benny.

On *Room 1411* Benny delivers a cheerfully punchy, if undistinguished, solo on baritone before turning in an assured clarinet solo. The same session produced *Blue* on which Benny's alto solo, while delightfully ingenuous, does owe rather more to 1920s dance music than to the hot jazz tradition.

Before leaving the studio the boys were fooling around, abetted by trombonist Tommy Dorsey who had arrived early for a different recording session. The record company man liked what he heard and insisted on recording it. Thus, a musicians' joke, a piece of what Jimmy McPartland called 'cod-Dixie', found its way into the record catalogues as *Shirt Tail Stomp*.

Towards the end of 1928 Benny made his first recordings under the pseudonym of The Whoopee Makers at a session which also saw the appearance of The Hotsy Totsy Gang, among other exotic names. Once more Benny played effective alto in addition to clarinet and on one tune, *I Couldn't If I Wanted To*, he also played soprano saxophone.

Through the winter of 1928-9 and on until he quit the Pollack band in the following summer, Benny was a frequent performer in the recording studios. Apart from numerous sessions with Pollack he made records with such exotically, or eccentrically, named groups as Goody and his Good Timers, the Dixie Daisies, the Lumberjacks, the Kentucky Grasshoppers and the Ten Black Diamonds. Two dates in 1929, both led by Red Nichols, brought Benny onto record with drummers Gene Krupa and Davey Tough. The session of 18 April, by Red Nichols and his Five Pennies, included Krupa who was already making a name for himself, and produced good solos by Benny on *Indiana*, *Dinah* and on one of two versions made of *On the Alamo*. Five days later, on a Louisiana Rhythm Kings date, Tough, at that time a much better known drummer, replaced Krupa.

Benny continued to associate with Red Nichols, both in the

recording studio and in a band the cornetist took into New York's Hollywood Restaurant towards the end of the year, but from early in 1930 he began a long working relationship with Ben Selvin. In the late spring of this year Benny also recorded for the first time with the man who had once ordered him to stop fooling with the band's instruments, Bix Beiderbecke.

This session was under the nominal leadership of Hoagy Carmichael and featured a truly all-star line-up. Apart from Benny and Bix the band included Ellingtonian Bubber Miley, the Dorsey brothers, Venuti and Lang, and Krupa. The tunes recorded were *Rockin' Chair* and *Barnacle Bill, the Sailor* which, however unlikely the material might seem, found everyone in cracking form with Goodman contributing a fine, hot solo.

Benny also found regular work on various radio shows emanating from New York City and at one time or another came under the batons of Paul Whiteman and André Kostelanetz. Such ventures as these, and those with Selvin's heavily pop-oriented music apart, Benny's recording dates were much more interesting to the jazz fan. Through 1930 and 1931 he recorded with Bix, Pee Wee Russell (about whom Benny once remarked to a student at Juillard, 'he's a great artist, but if you want to play like that, don't practise'), the brothers Dorsey and Teagarden, Eddie Condon, Fats Waller, Wingy Manone and Sterling Bose.

It was on a February 1931 date, headlined as by The Charleston Chasers, that Benny recorded versions of *Basin Street Blues* and *Beale Street Blues* on which he finally declared himself satisfied that he had placed on record examples of the style he had been trying to develop. Certainly, he is now playing with total confidence, something he had never lacked, and a new sophistication which overlays the fiery, urgent enthusiasm of his recordings of the previous four years. Here, he clearly demonstrates his command of his instrument and his musical environment.

In mid-1931, in England, a meeting between critic Edgar Jackson, then jazz editor of *Gramophone* magazine, and his American contributor, John Hammond, led to an association which would have a profound influence upon Benny Goodman's career. Jackson introduced Hammond to Spike Hughes of English Decca who expressed great interest in Benny Goodman whom Hammond had met but once and then only briefly. Hammond was a little surprised at Hughes's interest but decided that when the opportunity arose he would pay more attention to the clarinet-player. It would be a year or two before he managed to do so.

John Hammond's father was a successful lawyer and businessman while his mother was a Vanderbilt. Hammond was thus able to afford time and money in pursuing his passion for music in general and jazz in particular. Fortunately, he chose not to become a dilettante but instead worked hard at seeking out and promoting new talent. The number of musicians he helped bring to a wider world was astonishing and he is one of the three or four non-musicians to whom jazz owes an enormous debt. Undoubtedly, many of the people he assiduously promoted would have gained fame without his intervention but this does not in any way gainsay Hammond's importance. Apart from Benny Goodman, he boosted the careers of Billie Holiday, Count Basie, Teddy Wilson; and, outside jazz, he helped Bob Dylan, Aretha Franklin and Bruce Springsteen towards international fame.

Hammond's meeting with Goodman had been when Benny was contractor for Russ Columbo, a band in which Gene Krupa played. Towards the end of 1933 Hammond became associated with the English division of the Columbia Gramophone Company and was asked to set up some dates in America as Columbia's American operation was in financial deep-water. Among the musicians Hammond approached was Benny Goodman and despite some early diffidence on the clarinetist's part a date was set up. At the first of two sessions Goodman recorded *I Gotta Right to Sing the Blues* and *Ain't-Cha Glad?*, both with vocals by Jack Teagarden whose brother Charlie was also present with Teagarden again singing on two tunes recorded the following week. These were *Dr Heckle and Mr Jibe* and *Texas Tea Party (Call of the Freaks)*. On *I Gotta Right to Sing the Blues*, Benny's style is now fully developed. Even if the record is effectively Teagarden's, Benny uses his solo to stamp his authority on the proceedings.

Mannie Klein and Gene Krupa were on both dates, with Joe Sullivan playing piano on the first only. At the time Teagarden and Krupa were playing with the Mal Hallett band and, although Big Tea was happy to come into New York from Boston, Krupa took some convincing having had a run-in with Goodman when Benny was contracting for the Russ Columbo band in which Krupa was not allowed free rein to his talents. The first pairing of titles proved highly successful and, as John Hammond recalled in his autobiography, sales of 5,000 copies meant a hit in 1933.

Later in the same year Benny, again associating with John Hammond, made some significant records, not so much in terms of his own career but in those of the artists he accompanied. November, 1933 was a decidedly prolific month for him. He recorded with Red Norvo (playing marimba on this occasion), Annette Hanshaw whom he had already accompanied several times before, with Adrian Rollini and his Orchestra and with Steve Washington. But two sessions, spaced only three days apart, gave Benny the distinction of playing on the final recording session of the world's greatest blues singer and on the first session by a young woman who would become the world's greatest jazz singer.

Benny's playing on the Bessie Smith session, recorded on 24 November, is only fleetingly heard. Although claiming to be present on all four tunes, he can be heard only on *Gimme a Pigfoot*. It had been almost exactly two years since Bessie's previous record date but her voice had lost none of its powerful impact. Sadly, no other record producer saw fit to record her again during the final years of her life.

On 27 November, Benny recorded with Ethel Waters and two songs were produced: *I Just Couldn't Take It Baby* and *A Hundred Years From Today*. But it was the third tune recorded at this session, *Your Mother's Son-In-Law*, that was significant. The singer was a teenager named Billie Holiday. Rightly, later appreciations of this recording have concentrated upon the vocal but Benny Goodman's contribution should not be overlooked. Benny plays a positive lead in the opening ensemble and his liquid solo immediately before Billie's entry sets up an effective contrast with what follows. Despite her youth, Billie's voice already contains that astonishing maturity which completely overrides the banality of the lyric. Three weeks later the band returned to the studio for more tunes and once more Billie was there, this time to record *Riffin' the Scotch*.

Another fine singer Goodman recorded with during these winter months was Mildred Bailey and, indeed, as 1934 advanced there were a number of interesting sessions. On the Bailey date one non-vocal track, *Georgia Jubilee*, finds Benny very much in a supportive role to Coleman Hawkins' incomparable tenor saxophone and on

Junk Man it is clearly the singer who holds sway. Mildred Bailey's delicately ringing voice contrasts startlingly with Billie Holiday but her importance to jazz is never in question on this heavily blues influenced title. On *Ol' Pappy*, again a vocal track, Benny's role is more prominent and he emerges confidently from the shadow of Hawkins.

What with these records and radio shows Benny was always working but his personal ambitions were beginning to chafe at the restrictions of playing for other leaders on public engagements and not always being his own boss on record dates. On some, like the 'Bill Dodge' sessions in 1934, he hid behind a pseudonym and this too rankled. However, with the nation in the grip of the Depression, the times were not auspicious for launching any business venture. Then brother Harry came back to New York with the Pollack band and began working on Benny. Eventually, with the help of pianist Oscar Levant, Harry succeeded in convincing his kid brother that he should form his own permanent band.

Oscar Levant and Benny had met on a radio show and among the wise-cracking pianist's acquaintances was a showman named Billy Rose. A member of a syndicate which had made its loot during recently-ended Prohibition, Rose was planning to open a supper club at the old Manhattan Theatre. Rose agreed to listen to Benny's band and they were hired after a couple of auditions. Unfortunately, before the band could settle in, Billy Rose made the mistake of leaving the country for a while and on his return discovered that he had been elbowed aside. The new manager did not like Benny and his music and the elbow performed the same task with the musicians.

Before the axe fell, Benny recorded several titles with this band (the personnel fluctuating slightly over the few months of its existence). On *Nitwit Serenade*, a tune which owes more than a passing nod of acknowledgement to *Sugar Foot Stomp*, Benny sparkles against an energetic and well-rehearsed band. Benny's constant seeking for perfection through strict discipline, something instilled in him by his early tutor, Franz Schoepp, is already making itself apparent. On *Bugle Call Rag*, a tune which was to become a standby of later Goodman bands, Benny plays a driving solo over too-fussy drumming from Sammy Weiss while once again the ensemble passages are tight and cohesive.

The following month, September 1934, the band recorded a fine performance of Duke Ellington's *Solitude* with Benny in excellent form on a tune he seldom played. Indeed, throughout his career he only rarely performed Duke's works. Given the quality of this particular recording, the decision, if such it was, has to be regarded as unfortunate.

By November, as the Music Hall deal withered, the band was in cracking form. *Cokey* finds the ensemble passages being snappily performed even if Benny's short, middle-register solo is rather uninspired. However, at this same session, 26 November 1934, he demonstrated his total command with a powerful, fluent and inventive solo on *Music Hall Rag* (based on *The World is Waiting For the Sunrise*). Perhaps the sun was setting on this venture, but Benny was certainly riding high.

John Hammond now stepped in with the idea of taking an all-star band to Europe but on the eve of departure there were problems with bookings, and the project also encountered union difficulties in Great Britain and the deal fell through. Thus, British audiences lost the chance to hear a band whose full line-up makes mouth-watering reading, and incidentally, would have provided an astonishing example of a multi-racial band at a time when such aggregations were the stuff of dreams. The personnel booked for the aborted trip was: Red Allen, Doc Cheatham, Bill Coleman, Charlie Teagarden (t), J.C. Higginbotham, Will Bradley, Jack Teagarden (tb), Benny Goodman (cl), Benny Carter (as), Edgar Sampson, Chu Berry (ts), Teddy Wilson (p), Laurence Lucie (g), Hank Wayland (b), Gene Krupa (d) and Bessie Smith.

Russ Connor's assiduous researches have uncovered the existence of test pressings made by Columbia in October 1934 which appear to be by this band, or one very like it, but these apart this band remained a lost dream.

Benny's hopes of leading a permanent band were also on the point of being lost but in November he secured an audition for the National Biscuit Company's planned radio show. The programme was to run for three hours on Saturday nights with three bands sharing the honours. One was to be a sweet band, this spot went to Murray Kellner (Kel Murray); the second was to play latin-American music, this was Xaviar Cugat. The third spot was for a hot band and this was where Goodman was aiming albeit with little confidence. Despite his doubts the band was hired and so began a chain of events which would lead him to the very top.

At first the band was not quite right but minor personnel changes were made, including the hiring of Gene Krupa at the insistence of John Hammond. With further changes along the way, including the fine, if wayward, Bunny Berigan on trumpet, the band began to sound good and the charts by Edgar Sampson, Jimmy Mundy, Deane Kincaide and especially Fletcher Henderson appealed to musicians and listeners alike. The show went out across the nation and as a result was heard at different times of the night. At the time no one thought this important, if they thought about it at all.

The Nabisco radio show, entitled 'Let's Dance', ran from 1 December 1934 until 25 May 1935 and when it was over Benny was booked into New York's Roosevelt Hotel for what proved to be a disaster. The Roosevelt had been home for years to the Guy Lombardo band and the sedate, regular patrons disapproved of both the music of the Goodman band and the volume at which it was played. The waiters didn't care for it either, putting their fingers in their ears to show they were with the customers. The band was given notice on opening night. Having heard that record sales were good in California Benny agreed to a nationwide tour which would end with the opening of the Palomar Ballroom in Los Angeles in August 1935.

Before leaving New York, however, Benny attended a private party at the home of Mildred Bailey and her then husband Red Norvo. Also at the party was pianist Teddy Wilson. He and Benny played together and, as Benny would later recall, they hit it off right away.

In fact, Benny and Teddy had met before when the pianist was in Benny's band for record dates in May and October 1934. The meeting at Mildred Bailey's was, however, their first opportunity to test one another out. There can be no doubt about the musical empathy the two musicians felt for one another even if their personal relationship would generally remain a touch prickly. As Benny recalled in his 1939 autobiography (an 'as told to' collaboration with Irving Kolodin) 'it was something different than playing with the band, no matter how well it might be swinging, because here everything was close and intimate, with one fellow's ideas blending right in with the other's, and each of us getting a lift from what the other one was doing.'

In July, Benny recorded with the Teddy Wilson band which

accompanied Billie Holiday, now rapidly rising towards the pinnacle of her career. Three tunes were recorded, including *I Wished On the Moon* and the superb *What a Little Moonlight Can Do*.

Later that same month Benny and Teddy went into the studio and the first titles by the Benny Goodman Trio were recorded: *After You've Gone, Body and Soul, Who?* and *Someday, Sweetheart*.

Over the years these tunes would be played over and over again with *After You've Gone* and *Body and Soul* becoming, perhaps, over-used. These later performances included many that were excellent and it should not be seen as a devaluation of them to suggest that this first date was the best. With Gene Krupa replacing Carl Bellinger, a young relative of Mildred Bailey's, who had provided a decorous rhythmic background to the union of Benny and Teddy at the party, the formal recording session is filled with superb examples of that musical empathy. As Benny himself wrote, admittedly only three years later, 'they still stand out in my mind as some of the best playing we ever did together.' Decades on, he probably still thought the same – and rightly so.

Excellent as these recordings were, and despite their enormous success with the record-buying public, for the moment the thought of Teddy becoming a regular member of the entourage never arose. Black and white musicians might play together in private, or at a few tiny jazz clubs where only *afficionados* were on hand, or on record dates where colour mattered not at all. The dance dates which provided bands like Goodman's with work were a very different matter. Black bands were fine and so too were white bands, but mixed bands meant trouble.

Trouble of a different kind awaited the Benny Goodman band as it began its national tour. Reaction was only so-so in Pittsburgh, Columbus, Toledo, Milwaukee and no one was expecting much when the tour reached Denver. This was for a four-week stint at Elitch's Gardens, a three-dances-for-a-dime joint. From the start Benny and the dancehall manager were at loggerheads; Benny's already developed tendancy to speak his mind with no regard for tact was a major factor in poor relations. The manager called Willard Alexander, then managing the band for MCA, and asked to be released from the contract. Alexander asked a few questions, then spoke to Benny. The central problem was not the fact that the manager at Elitch's Gardens disliked the music (in fact, he hated it) but that each number was lasting so long that the customers' dimes were buying too much hostess-time. By shortening the band's numbers and borrowing charts for a string of waltzes, Benny averted a complete disaster but everyone was relieved when it was time to leave Denver. Not that things improved very much until California.

The band's appearance in San Franciso, was somewhat better, but by the time they reached the Palomar Ballroom in Los Angeles no one held out much hope for the future. They were wrong, and of considerable importance in their error was the time-zoning of the United States which meant that the band's spot on the 'Let's Dance' radio show had come on at peak listening time in California, rather than after midnight when the kids were in bed, or at least unable to listen to the radio in those pre-tranny days. Additionally, a local radio deejay, Al Jarvis, had been playing Goodman's records extensively on his 'Make Believe Ballroom' show (a format and title later adopted by Martin Block on the East Coast).

Opening on 21 August at the Palomar, Benny began with the band's sweetest dance tunes and while applause was polite it was far from enthusiastic. The fact that the Palomar's management had tried to scratch the band after hearing of the Denver debacle made everyone edgy. Then, thinking that this might well be the last time they would play together, Benny called up one of Fletcher Henderson's arrangements. The tune was *Sugar Foot Stomp,* a number featuring a searing solo from Bunny Berigan that ripped through the ballroom. This was what the kids had come here for, and they went wild.

Far from cancelling out, the Palomar extended the four-week engagement and the band stayed in California until October with local dates flooding in. From the coast the band dropped down into Texas and was then offered the Joseph Urban room at the Congress Hotel in Chicago. On the surface this was not the best gig in the country as the hotel was striving to recover its popularity after being hit by an outbreak of food-poisoning during the World's Fair.

Additionally, despite the success in Los Angeles, there was no significant carry-over of enthusiasm as records and radio remotes were heard only by limited numbers of people. But, perhaps as a result of the band's new confidence, they carried the Congress Hotel so successfully that the engagement was extended again and again. In all, they played there for about half a year. The band continued to broadcast extensively, attracting widespread attention and a small army of fans. For Benny to have made it big anywhere in the United States was an enormous achievement, to make it this big in the town where he had been born into a poor immigrant family, just twenty-five years before, was a very sweet moment.

Sweet as this undoubtedly was, the best was yet to come.

Chapter Three

Listening to recordings by the Benny Goodman band of the 1930s through to the early 1940s raises interesting reflections on some of those hoary old problems attached to many bands of the period. Many of them used charts which lasted much longer than the three-minute side of a 78 rpm record and the sound of these bands on studio recordings is often very different from that heard by the fans at the time in dancehalls and hotels across the nation. Fortunately, as time has passed numerous recordings made from broadcasts have emerged and Goodman has been especially well-featured in this manner. In Goodman's case, the arrangements are relatively restricting and the band adheres to them although there are certain differences most notably in the attack both of the ensemble and the individual section passages. With the added spur of a live audience Benny's soloists, while confined to the allocated space, frequently play with much more bite.

The studio recordings, however, still retain much appeal even if, sometimes, it is for odd moments rather than their complete span. For example, in the 1935 studio recording of *King Porter Stomp* Bunny Berigan's solo shines brightly in a band which occasionally appears to lack confidence in itself.

The band which recorded, say, Fletcher Henderson's *Down South Camp Meeting* in 1936 is much more relaxed. Perhaps it lacks the plangent swing of Henderson's own band on the same tune recorded two years earlier; and there is certainly no one in Goodman's trumpet section to match Red Allen, but then no one in Henderson's band could equal Goodman's solo.

During the band's stint at the Congress Hotel national recognition was inevitable as the enthusiasm of audiences began to percolate through to the non-showbiz pages of newspapers, much as would the adulation of the Beatles a quarter-century later. *Life* magazine's journalists engaged in feats of semantic gymnastics as they tried convincing their readers that 'Swing' was somehow a more refined white version of the now-dead black music known as 'jazz'. The somewhat more hip readers of *Metronome*, asked to vote for the first time in a 'best swing band' category, unhesitatingly chose Goodman.

The infectious enthusiasm of the band and audience on those old radio show broadcasts make the swing 'craze' more understandable despite the grim circumstances in which many lived in the mid-1930s. In fact, while President Roosevelt's statement, that one-third of the nation was ill-clad, ill-fed and ill-housed was true, many people were not doing so badly that they couldn't work up an appetite for musical treats.

While still at the Congress, Benny brought in Teddy Wilson for a Sunday dance-cum-concert organised by Helen Oakley and others. A similar engagement had been widely publicized in *Time* magazine and Goodman was understandably nervous but the appearance of a black musician as one-third of the Trio passed without adverse comment. This encouraged Benny and John Hammond to consider asking Teddy to become a permanent member. To ease him in he was hired as intermission pianist, while the Trio performed as part of the floor show.

In later years, aware of Benny's reputation as a hard businessman, Teddy Wilson commented to writer Nat Hentoff: 'I knew of the pressures that were pulling Benny the other way. Guys in the music business were telling him he'd ruin his career if he hired me. They weren't necessarily antiblack; they were businessmen.' Well, so too was Benny, but he was also acutely aware of the musical empathy he felt for Wilson and in the end that was what won.

By mid-1936 Benny and the band were appearing on the Elgin Watch Company's radio show and when the show moved to New York they went too. After playing some dates around New York the band was hired to appear in a movie and left for California and a return engagement at the Palomar.

The movie, *The Big Broadcast of 1937*, turned out to be the least important event on this trip. John Hammond, ever attuned to new music and musicians (he had first heard the Count Basie band while listening on his car radio in the parking lot at the Congress during Benny's engagement there), sent Benny down to the Paradise Café in Los Angeles, to listen to the band led by a gifted young multi-instrumentalist named Lionel Hampton.

Benny did as Hammond suggested, was knocked out by Hampton's playing of the vibraphone, at that time still a novelty instrument in other hands, went back the next evening with Teddy Wilson and Gene Krupa and the Benny Goodman Quartet was born. Within days the four made their first recording taking advantage of a session set up for the full orchestra. One title was cut, *Moonglow*, but others followed in the next few days. At a session headlined by Wilson the quartet plus four more from the band recorded *You came To My Rescue* and *Here's Love In Your Eyes;* then the Quartet made two more titles a couple of days later. These tunes were *Dinah* and *Vibraphone Blues* on which Lionel also sang (although perhaps he shouldn't have). He also sang but did not play on a Trio title recorded at the same session: *Exactly Like You.* The success of these records made Hampton's membership of the organisation merely a matter of time.

The sound of the Quartet was quite different from that of the Trio, whether on ballads or up-tempo numbers. Krupa fitted in well with Goodman and Wilson on Trio performances, subduing his natural exuberence so as not to overpower yet never letting blandness set in. When Lionel Hampton was added there was always greater tension as if the others were waiting to see which side of his volatile personality would be on display. When he was in his Dr Jekyll-mode the subtleties of the Goodman-Wilson partnership were enhanced; when Mr Hyde had the upper hand it was Krupa who responded and if, at times, Wilson faded a little during such tear-ups, Goodman dug deeper into his hot repertoire and produced some of his best performances.

Late in 1936 Goodman participated in several rewarding recording sessions including one with Ella Fitzgerald, then singing with her mentor Chick Webb and his Orchestra. Contractual problems led to suppression of the records for a number of years but eventually *Goodnight, My Love, Take Another Guess* and *Did You Mean It?* were released. On the first of these titles in particular, Ella highlights the wide gulf between herself and Benny's usual singers.

Benny doubled the black contingent in the entourage in November of this year when Lionel Hampton drove to New York in a battered old car complete with vibraphone and new wife Gladys. The story goes that Benny sent the rail fare but Gladys put her foot down firmly, as she was wont to do, insisted that if Lionel went she went too and that meant marriage and *that* meant the biggest ring in the jewelry store. Hence the beat-up Chevy.

Early in 1937 another new addition to the band was Harry James who had been with Ben Pollack. As Ziggy Elman had joined the previous September Goodman now had his most famous trumpet section: James, Elman and Chris Griffin who stayed together for two years and so shared their work that each became equally adept at leading and soloing. This subordination of personalities to the greater needs of the band helped enormously and the section had an assertive power that was noticeably absent in all the other white bands of the time, and not a few of the black bands would have benefited from such a team if they could usually cut them as individual soloists. And, although none of these three could measure up to the solo abilities of Bunny Berigan, Benny probably considered that freedom from the problems which came in the wake of Berigan's drinking was sufficient compensation. Generally, while with Benny, neither Harry James nor Ziggy indulged in the often tasteless performances which marred their playing when they later led bands of their own. The signs are there, but for the most part they played hotter and better with Benny Goodman than at any other times in their careers.

By now Benny was nationally famous. His faintly owlish, bespectacled face, topped by dark, slicked-back hair, stared out from posters, newspapers and sheet music. Even his voice, a strange combination of gruff low-pitched gargles and occasional high-pitched squeaks, became known to millions thanks to the radio broadcasts.

His personal characteristics – determined perfectionism in his playing and caution over money – were now gaining him additional reputations among musicians. His insistence on perfection extended beyond himself to every member of his band and rehearsals were occasions to be feared. On-stage, if a musician played below par, or did something else Benny did not like, there would be no tongue-lashing: that would have been unprofessional conduct; instead, Benny developed the 'ray'. This was a basilisk stare which focussed at

29

a point three feet behind the unfortunate recipient's head and caused all but the toughest to quail in his seat.

He tended to think in an impersonal way, which led to increased remoteness from the other musicians who were usually highly gregarious. As Bud Freeman recalled: 'Maybe Benny was impervious to the feelings of other people but I don't think that he's essentially a bad guy. I think he's just the kind who gets in a sort of fog about things.'

The fog led to several tales, one of which has Benny climbing into a cab after a concert and sitting there in silence for several minutes. Eventually, the driver turned to look into the back of his still stationary vehicle. 'Well?' he asked. Benny promptly snapped out of a light doze, climbed out and asked how much he owed for the ride.

His care with money troubled tenor saxophonist Vido Musso (again recalled by Bud Freeman) who trimmed his reed by burning it around the edge of a 50c piece. Benny would take the coin from Vido, trim his own reed, then pocket the half dollar. At the same time Benny had fallen into the habit of leaving his clarinet for Vido to dismantle and clean. Growing weary of this task, and the regular loss of half a dollar, Vido began to exchange his clarinet for Benny's. He did it, piece by piece, over a few weeks until he owned Benny's instrument. Benny, apparently, never noticed.

A reputation of a different kind was growing with the public and Benny was dubbed the King of Swing (although it has been suggested that the title was first bestowed upon Gene Krupa as part of an advertising campaign for Slingerland Drums). Perhaps the black musicians of the time were rightly less than enthusiastic at the success of white bands; nevertheless, few would deny that popular music of the day benefited greatly from the injection of jazz phrasing which was encouraged by the popularity of Swing. Yet there was always the faint fear that it was all a bubble which would quickly burst. That fear was banished, at least for some years, when Benny was appearing nightly at the Madhattan Room at New York's Hotel Pennsylvania. Doubling was commonplace, after all work wasn't so plentiful that engagements could be turned down. This particular doubling was at the Paramount Theatre where the band was booked to provide the live music between screenings of the new Claudette Colbert movie, *Maid of Salem*.

When the band turned up for the morning show there were

already hundreds of teenagers standing in line. By the time the elevating stage rose into view carrying the whole band, already into its theme, *Let's Dance,* roars of eager approval were echoing around the theatre. Long before the band's part of the programme was over kids were dancing in the aisles and the management was anxiously trying to quell what they were convinced was an incipient riot.

In a sense it was a riot, one of public acclaim for a popular musician which was almost completely unknown at the time and was certainly unknown in such proportions. The Paramount engagement thrust the Benny Goodman band firmly into the consciousness of the wider public and for the first time jazz was accepted as a form of popular entertainment. Hitherto, jazz had been written about (if it was written about at all) as though it were some kind of plague visited upon an unsuspecting nation by a vengeful god. Churchmen, psychiatrists, doctors and politicians (all of whom should have known better, but then, of course, they never do) joined in the attack. But that was when jazz was the property of black Americans and any whites who played or enthused were dismissed as degenerate. Now, the kids shagging and lindyhopping in the aisles of the Paramount, and soon in every dancehall across the nation, were white, middle-class and *respectable.* They had to be, they were the sons and daughters of churchmen, psychiatrists, doctors and politicians, to say nothing of newspaper advertisers and proprietors. Knowing on which side its bread was buttered, the establishment prepared to accept jazz. Well, not exactly. They prepared to accept 'swing', having taken care to build artificial dividing lines between the two; lines that were all too often distinguished by colour.

But, whatever the reason, and doubtless no one in the Goodman band at the time philosophised over it for very long, Swing was the thing and Benny was its King. Sidemen in the bands became household names, were mobbed and fêted; they became rich and married movie stars and their every move was reported. When those moves were between bands the fans charted arrivals and departures as assiduously as any baseball or football supporter.

In the Goodman band during this period the personnel underwent several changes but until early 1938 few of these changes had an appreciable effect upon the sound. Benny's insistence upon lengthy rehearsals and a high degree of perfection in the playing (if not in the private lives) of his men contributed to this. Yet, taken section by section, the band had many drawbacks when set against other big bands of the era.

The trumpet section as already mentioned had fire and attack yet neither as a section nor as individual soloists did it come up to the standards of the top half dozen black bands. The trombones, which over the years in question included Vernon Brown, Red Ballard and Murray McEachern (who turned up decades later as a much respected and sought-after lead alto saxophonist), were competent but never inspired and could be weak on solos. The same general comment can be made of the saxophone section although the gritty tenor of Vido Musso was a definite plus. The rhythm section was individually sound, especially when Jess Stacy was on the piano stool; and if Harry Goodman was not as good as his successors, Allan Reuss was one of the best section guitarists around. Krupa provided a solid foundation and was a much better timekeeper than his detractors would allow. Nevertheless, as a section the rhythm players faded into the woodwork when set against the freewheeling flow of Basie's All-American Rhythm Section.

Most of the records of airshots issued in recent years include numerous examples of the fire the band could display outside the occasionally stifling surroundings of the recording studios. Yet there are many fine moments from the studio dates, especially when listened to again on good quality reproductions. One of the beneficiaries of such reissues is pianist Jess Stacy whose contributions to the rhythm section were not always clearly audible on the old 78s.

Jimmy Mundy's arrangement of *Bugle Call Rag* is an interesting example of the band's progress. On 21 August, 1936, a version was recorded which received only limited issue as Benny was not too happy with the result. About three months later on 5 November, the tune was recorded again. This time the trumpet section had changed from Sterling Bose, Pee Wee Erwin and Chris Griffin to Zeke Zarchy, Ziggy Elman and Griffin. Otherwise the band is essentially the same (the saxophone section had dropped a tenor player). The new trumpet section's zest is noticeable but more than anything else it is the improved familiarity with the arrangement shown by the entire band which enhances this second attempt.

By the beginning of 1937, the further change, which brought in Harry James, had occurred. Already the strength of the new trumpet section is apparent. *I Want To Be Happy*, a Fletcher

Henderson arrangement, recorded on 14 January, admirably demonstrates the progress. This same session also produced excellent performances by Benny and Jess Stacy on the unpromising material of *Chlo-e,* again a Henderson arrangement. It was at Benny's insistence that Henderson had turned his talents to lightweight popular songs, having previously favoured working on jazz standards. There is no doubt that this was a wise move. Apart from the simple commercial factor of giving the public the kind of music it was showing a preference for, it also extended Fletcher Henderson's range and his importance to jazz and especially his importance to Benny Goodman.

Benny did not rely solely upon the arrangements of Henderson, Mundy and Sampson, of course. He used Fletcher's brother Horace, who arranged *Big John Special* and *Dear Old Southland,* and Mary Lou Williams contributed fine work of which *Roll 'Em,* which she also wrote, is perhaps the best known. Even Harry James supplied an occasional chart, *Peckin'* being an excellent example.

Nevertheless, despite the work of all these arrangers, the power is clearly Benny himself. The fact that his contributions were restricted almost exclusively to playing should not obscure the fact that the singlemindedness with which he had set out to become the best clarinet-player was also driving him to be the leader of the best band. For Benny, being best meant being the most successful, which accounts for the fact that he never attempted to go down the road signposted by the likes of Basie. Although there were limited numbers of white musicians around who could have made an attempt at playing the way the Basie crew did, Benny never hired them. They would not have given him what he wanted from his own band. For one thing, they would have made a different sound.

What is indisputable is that *his* band sounded exactly the way Benny wanted. And with an ear well-tuned to the cash registers, he also knew what the fans wanted and he gave it to them. But, there were limits to how far he would go and they were sometimes strained by the gallery-rousing efforts of some of the band, and of Gene Krupa in particular.

Benny's ideal musician was defined by him in his ghosted autobiography. 'What I admire most in a musician . . . is really good ideas – the ability to say something with his playing. After that comes competence . . . the ability to read off a part at sight. . . .' Nothing there about inspiration or improvisational skills or a feeling for the blues. These were not essential factors in the Goodman sound; Benny the perfectionist was always uneasy with the unexpected.

Early in 1938 Benny and the band reached a new pinnacle with the decision to make a concert appearance at New York's Carnegie Hall. They had made another movie the previous summer and *Hollywood Hotel* opened on 15 January, the day on which the engagement at the Madhattan Room ended. The following day came Carnegie Hall. Concerts were relatively unknown for jazz groups and if Carnegie Hall was not exactly virgin territory it was still the most prestigious gig in town.

Despite the successes at the Paramount this was thought to be different, but doubts disappeared when the hall was sold out on the day booking began. Goodman was still nervous however and when the time came to kick off he reputedly struck the wrong tempo. In fact, listening to the recording, the opening couple of minutes sound reasonably relaxed but this was not the kind of thing Krupa and the rest of the boiler-room gang wanted. Twice the drummer rattles out an explosive suggestion on tempo and the crowd's roar of approval undoubtedly helped settle a few nerves. Despite earlier comments on the general stability of Krupa's timekeeping, the Carnegie concert does contain more than a handful of irregularities and several instances where tunes were performed too fast, especially the small group numbers. Overall, however, any quibbling is beside the point. By the end of the evening the crowd was solidly behind the band and when Krupa opened up on *Sing, Sing, Sing* it would have taken a collapsing balcony to dampen the enthusiasm. True, almost everything played that night was played better on other occasions but the air of this being a special event pervades everything. The only tune that was never given a better reading was, in fact, *Sing, Sing, Sing* and that was due entirely to an unscheduled and unexpected solo by Jess Stacy who produced the one thing so greatly lacking in the Goodman band up to this time – inspiration.

That later generations could hear this and all the other events of that momentous evening is due to Albert Marks, the husband of Benny's one-time singer Helen Ward. Marks recorded the proceedings on a single overhead microphone and gave the resulting acetates to Benny who put them in a closet and forgot about them for a dozen years. By the time he discovered them again the record industry had moved on apace and the new long-playing records allowed the release of the concert. In time they became the best-selling jazz records, a position they may well still hold as their regular re-releasing ensures that no generation need be without them.

The past few years had been very good for Benny and his band but changes loomed. These did not come about with the feared bursting of the swing era 'bubble' but from within as the band's most popular member locked horns with his boss.

Gene Krupa's popularity with the public met with Benny's disapproval and he was similarly disenchanted with Gene's conflicting views on musical policy. Benny began to sit on the drummer's spectacular solo features; the crowds disapproved and so did Gene. With the benefit of hindsight the rift appears inevitable but at Carnegie Hall on 16 January 1938 no one could have guessed that the break was only a matter of weeks away.

Chapter Four

'Being a part of this band was the fulfilment of a dream for any young musician. . . . For all that Benny did for music, for jazz, for musicians, and for me, I, for one, doff my cap in a salute of sincere appreciation.' So spoke Gene Krupa to Shapiro and Hentoff, the two Nats who compiled *Hear Me Talkin' To Ya*. Clearly, whatever the irritations that led to Krupa quitting Goodman, the passage of time had cooled tempers.

The break came on-stage at the Earle Theatre in Philadelphia where the band was booked for a one-week engagement from 26 February 1938. The crowd was yelling for solos from Gene but Benny refused. Gene shrugged at the mob, clearly indicating that he wanted to meet their demands but Benny wouldn't play ball. On odd occasions when Gene did have a short solo, Benny managed to convey an impression of total boredom. When the Earle Theatre gig ended on 3 March, Gene quit the band.

In the light of what happened to the Goodman band after Krupa's departure the drummer's importance must not be overestimated. The band went from strength to strength and if it did not always sound better it certainly sounded different. Musical matters aside, no one can seriously doubt the value of Gene to the band during the formative years. His enthusiasm was constant and infectious and he undoubtedly attracted a great deal of attention to a unit which had no other charismatic personality in its ranks, nor even fronting it for Benny could never be thought magnetic. This facet of Krupa was appreciated by Benny at later, cooler times. 'There was always Gene and his "showmanship" for the writers to talk about,' Benny wrote. 'Even if they didn't have any idea what a great drummer he was.'

But with Gene gone Benny wasted no time in hiring a replacement. Indeed, the speed with which it was done suggests he had made contingency plans. The man who came in was Benny's (and Gene's) old friend, Davey Tough. For a time the fans disapproved. Gone was the flash and visual excitement, gone too was the non-stop thunderous roar of Krupa's piston-like attack. In its place came the kind of drumming that musicians like best but which those fans who listen with their eyes and feet tend to dismiss. Tough played with a fluid dexterity that brought a lift to the band and to individual soloists that came much closer to the best of the black drummers than was achieved by any other white musician of the time.

Unfortunately, the Goodman band never really had a chance to build a new style for itself on this kind of drumming because, however effective he might be on-stage, Tough's private life was a shambles and soon proved too much for Benny – and eventually for Tough himself. A highly literate man, with a genuine gift for writing and a deep interest in the arts, Tough drank recklessly. His marriage to a pretty dancer, as diminutive as himself, was not as entirely stabilising as it might have been because Casey Majors was black and the early 1940s were not yet the time for mixed marriages in America. At regular and increasingly frequent intervals, Davey Tough's drinking took control but he still managed a few rewarding spells with various bands (especially Woody Herman's in the mid-1940s). He died one night in 1948 when he fell in the street and cracked open his head.

There were other changes in the band apart from the drum chair, and to some extent all affected its sound. Art Bernstein replaced Harry Goodman on bass and Fletcher Henderson came in on piano. Much has been made of Goodman's success being built upon Henderson's arrangements with hints, if not plain accusations, that this was somehow underhand. Certainly, Benny was always a businessman but reflection suggests that the deal was adequate even if Henderson was in a financial bind at the time. Benny's later hiring of Henderson for the vacant piano stool and later still his work for the Fletcher Henderson Fund displays a genuine concern and it would be both churlish and unfounded to imply, as have some writers, that guilt was a motivating force.

Harry James also left, at the end of 1938, and the fans must have thought their world was falling apart. But, for those with ears, a man was about to join the band who would bring with him a quality it had hitherto lacked – true genius.

Once more it was John Hammond who made the introduction although this time Benny must be forgiven for thinking, as he did, that Hammond had lost his reason. Finding Lionel Hampton (and his assiduous promotion of Billie Holiday) showed that Hammond had ears but he also needed a kind of blindness when it came to Charlie Christian.

Hammond recalled the first time he met Christian (it was at Mildred Bailey's instigation) at the Ritz Café in Oklahoma City: he was a 'tall young man, thin, dark, and wearing a purple shirt and bright yellow shoes.' Some days later Charlie arrived at the Columbia recording studios in Los Angeles where Hammond was supervising a Goodman session. He still had on the yellow shoes and contrasting shirt. He also wore a big hat and was lugging large chunks of amplification machinery. Benny gave him short shrift but that night, at the Victor Hugo Restaurant in Beverley Hills, Hammond smuggled Charlie and his equipment onto the bandstand during the intermission trusting that even Benny wouldn't publicly vent his displeasure.

When Benny returned to the stand he was mightily displeased, especially as Charlie still wore what Hammond was rapidly realising was his only set of clothes. Benny fixed Hammond with a glare that would have removed paint, counted off *Rose Room*, a tune he guessed Charlie wouldn't know, and prepared to put this upstart and John Hammond firmly in their place. The rest, of course, is history. As soon as Benny indicated Charlie should take a solo the young unknown began a brilliant twenty-five chorus improvisation that had the crowd and Benny yelling with astonished approval. That performance of *Rose Room* lasted forty-five minutes and if ever there was a case for a time machine to go back to record missed moments in the history of jazz this must be it.

Charlie joined the entourage and like Teddy Wilson and Lionel Hampton before him he too was usually confined to the small group. This was a decided advantage as he could always be heard to superb effect, although on the few occasions he was recorded with the full band he was never overshadowed. The Benny Goodman Sextet, as the small group now was, made Benny's greatest contribution to jazz. The exposure granted to Charlie Christian was greater than if he had joined any other orchestra. Charlie was deeply involved at Minton's in New York, the after-hours club where the younger jazzmen gathered and where new sounds were being heard. This new music heralded the end of the Swing Era and thus Charlie succeeded in making a permanent mark on jazz.

Almost any performance by the Sextet can be cited as a fine example of Charlie's work, indeed it is virtually impossible to think of anything he did that does not bear the signs and sounds of his genius.

Among the studio recorded sessions were *Till Tom Special*, on which he can be heard demonstrating an early example of bebop phrasing, *Wholly Cats, Gone With What Wind*, a fine instance of his blues influences, and *A Smo-o-o-oth One*.

Some years later, once again thanks to the advent of long-playing records, the warm-up to this last title was released and shows how Charlie built up the deceptively simple riff which eventually became the tune recorded later that day when Benny arrived (although Benny's name appears as composer). Entitled *Waiting For Benny*, this and other available warm-up sessions provide one of the best introductions to Charlie Christian's innovative and creative capacities and only these and the later private recordings made at Minton's come close to giving a flavour of what that first meeting at the Victor Hugo must have been like.

Examples of Charlie's work with the big band also exist and the two available versions of *Solo Flight* are both instructive and delightful. Beginning life as *Chonk, Charlie, Chonk, Solo Flight* is constructed as a miniature concerto with the orchestra playing a decidedly subordinate role to his simple, yet brilliant, solo.

Late in 1940, Goodman rehearsed an octet which never made any commercial sides but many years later acetates of the rehearsals turned up and were subsequently released on record. This line-up had Benny and Charlie playing with members of the Basie band: Lester Young, Buck Clayton, Freddie Green, Walter Page, Jo Jones and the Count himself. (Although some sources suggest a slightly different personnel this sounds right.) Like other splendid ideas in jazz this was never pursued but these recordings at least give a glimpse of what might have been. Benny plays very well, clearly benefiting from such a rhythm section but the honours must go to Charlie and Lester Young. Later formal dates were good but by then the Count's men had dropped out and while Cootie Williams was a good alternative to Buck Clayton, Georgie Auld clearly could not be compared in any way with Lester Young.

Although not the originator of amplified guitar-playing, Christian was certainly a pioneer and the one who brought the technique to the public and ensured its full flowering. That some of his successors outside the jazz world chose to make uses of his creations that concern themselves with things other than skill and style and, for want of a better word, class, should not detract one iota from his significance.

Unfortunately, fame was something Charlie couldn't handle. Working every evening with the Goodman band, jamming through till morning with his friends, exploring the delights of female company, and sampling a better class of booze to the bootleg corn whiskey on which he had been weaned, his constitution, never very strong, cracked up and he fell ill. Hospital should have been the right place to be, but it wasn't because his friends, and they were many, came to visit and brought with them a few of the supplies they thought he might need: booze, women and grass. Charlie took this medicine much more readily than that prescribed by his doctors and he never left the hospital. Just short of two years after joining Benny Goodman at the Victor Hugo Restaurant in Los Angeles, Charlie Christian died in Seaview Sanitarium, Staten Island on 2 March 1942. Estimates of his age vary but he was no older than twenty-six.

During the early 1940s Benny hired other black musicians, among them Cootie Williams who made the small group up into a Septet and also played in the full band's trumpet section. For a while Benny had Big Sid Catlett on drums although given his objections to Krupa's grandstanding this was asking for trouble. A spectacular soloist, Big Sid had a penchant for wearing suits of vivid green with broad chalk stripes, or even, on occasion, green plaid. Benny must have gone temporarily blind. In later years, speaking of Catlett's short stay with the band, Benny remarked, somewhat obscurely: 'It's always been one of my enigmas – drummers.' (Billie Holiday had her own, much earthier, view of Catlett. 'They don't call him Big Sid just because he's six feet four,' she said.)

Another change brought Johnny Guarnieri in on piano but he

failed to impress his leader. 'When I first joined Benny,' Johnny later recalled, 'he called me "Fletcher" for three months before he could remember my name.' Given that Johnny was white while Fletcher Henderson wasn't suggests that Goodman's notorious forgetfulness was either at crisis point or he was indulging in a little private war. Indeed, his declaration that Johnny was the worst pianist he'd had since Frankie Froeba and that he didn't like his habit of 'imitating' other pianists indicates that Benny might have been going through a crisis of a different sort. Certainly, Benny's health was plagueing him and sciatica became a recurring problem. The band was also under pressure from others as the Swing Era demanded more and more big bands. With the Dorsey brothers, Artie Shaw, Woody Herman, to say nothing of Gene Krupa's and Harry James's among the thousands, poaching of musicians became epidemic.

There were almost as many black bands around as white, even if they were not getting the plum radio and hotel jobs. Teddy Wilson had left to form a highly competent and very musicianly group which never made it commercially and in 1940, while Benny was temporarily disbanded due to his sciatica, Lionel Hampton also left. As with Harry James, he took with him Benny's blessing, advice and some financial support in return for a piece of the action.

During 1941 Benny had to find a new girl singer when Helen Forrest left to join Harry James. Benny's choice of singers although uninspired seems on the whole to have been rather better than that of many of his contemporaries. Helen Ward, the first important singer he had, was a considerable step above the pretty canary in a party dress who stood in front of too many of the big bands. Martha Tilton was not really an improvement although she certainly did not deserve her peremptory firing. This came about when Benny, in a devastating display of tactlessness, obviously irritated that several members of the band had handed in their notices, turned to Martha and said, 'Well, you might as well go too.'

His attitude towards his girl singers was consistent if nothing else. Decades later, while rehearsing at his Connecticut home for a TV appearance, he and some musicians plus one of his former singers, were playing on the patio in the afternoon sunshine. Time wore on, the sun sank lower, and eventually the lady could no longer give her full attention to the job in hand. 'Don't you think it's getting a little chilly?' she asked. Benny looked up from his clarinet, thought for a moment, shivered, nodded agreement, then stood up and went into the house. A few moments later he came back, now clad in a warm sweater, picked up his clarinet and continued with the rehearsal.

Benny had fixed musical ideas about how a girl singer should sound. Before hiring Helen Forrest he had auditioned a young lady named Anita Colton, rebuked her for her disregard of the melody, and sent her packing. With a new name, Anita O'Day, this young woman soon proved that she did not need Benny when she was hired by Gene Krupa and rose to deserved fame as one of the finest singers ever to grace the world of jazz.

It was in August 1941, while filling an engagement at the Sherman Hotel in Chicago, that Benny stayed at the Ambassador. A singing trio included a girl who caught his attention. (He had pulled Martha Tilton out of a vocal group so his ears were certainly sharp enough to know who was doing what in such outfits.) This new girl was Norma Egstrom who quickly became Peggy Lee. She gave the band a further asset and soon had hit recordings to help boost earnings and popularity. There was *Elmer's Tune,* her first record with the band, then *My Old Flame* and *How Deep Is the Ocean* while *Why Don't You Do Right?* became a massive seller.

Benny also found a drummer who proved to be one of the most adept in both big band and small group settings, although Nick Fatool also contrived to become one of the most underrated drummers in jazz.

The sound of the band Benny led in 1941 and 1942 was markedly different thanks in part to the new men in its ranks but principal credit for the changes must go to arrangers Eddie Sauter and Mel Powell. Powell was a very young piano-player who entered the band after Teddy Wilson had made a temporary reappearance. Unlike the earlier arrangers, much of whose work was better suited to a looser band than Benny's, Sauter and Powell approached their task rather differently. The results have a cleaner sound and while there is never the pent-up drive of the pre-Carnegie Hall band, there is no lack of swing and Benny himself certainly sounds at ease on such numbers as Sauter's *Clarinet à la King* which finds the leader at his relaxed best. In some respects the construction of the piece is almost classical and approaches that of a trio: clarinet, rhythm and orchestra. *The Earl* is one of Powell's numbers (he composed it too) and the band here sounds slightly more relaxed but swings surprisingly well having no dummer on the commercial release. This was when Big Sid Catlett was in the ranks and either Benny dumped him or merely preferred the sound of the band this way, depending upon which version of events is believed. Benny is in good form on this and also on another Powell composition and arrangement, *Mission to Moscow*, made just before the pianist moved on.

When America entered World War Two Benny was rejected for service as a result of his chronic sciatica but the band did its bit for the boys overseas by recording V-Discs which had the added benefit of preserving (unofficially, since the records should have been destroyed) the sound of the band during the long and ultimately highly damaging strike called by the American Federation of Musicians. The strike, more precisely a ban on participation in recording sessions, helped boost the careers of many singers who were unaffected by the union's action.

One young man who was helped in this way was Frank Sinatra who had been discovered by Harry James and came to prominence with the Tommy Dorsey band. Sinatra's solo debut had begun a new trend in popular music and his first major booking was at the Paramount Theatre in New York where he shared the bill with Benny and the band. It was during the Paramount engagement that Benny's unusual view of his musicians came to the attention of trumpet-player Yank Lawson (recalled by Bud Freeman many years later). The band had to steal off-stage after the lights had dimmed and in the dark saxophonist Hank D'Amico fell into the pit, dropping his clarinet in the process. As Yank helped Hank, Benny rushed for the instrument. 'The clarinet's okay,' he called. 'It's okay!'

This Paramount date with Sinatra came at the end of 1942 and earlier that year Benny had surprised everyone by renouncing his bachelor status (if anyone so fully-wedded to his music can be so termed) and had married Alice Duckworth who was John Hammond's sister.

Early in 1943 Benny and Alice, and her three children from a previous marriage, were in California where the band was appearing in a movie, *The Gang's All Here,* and he stayed on for a while as their first child was due. Rachel, who was born on 2 May, in Los Angeles, would eventually become a concert pianist.

Also in California in 1943 was Gene Krupa, then riding high with the best of his several bands. This one had Roy Eldridge in the trumpet section and the singer whom Benny had turned down flat, thus displaying a marked lack of perception – but maybe Anita O'Day's style would never have fitted into the Goodman sound. Krupa's California trip proved much less enjoyable than Benny's as he ended up in a San Francisco courtroom from where he went to prison on a drugs-related charge which was later dismissed – but not until after he had served his sentence and his band had folded.

Goodman was one of the few people to visit Gene in prison and later that year, when the drummer was back home in New York and thinking seriously of quitting the performing side of the music business, it was Benny who talked him into returning to the drums. More the point, Benny wanted him in *his* band. Cagey at public reaction, Gene agreed to go along on a tour of USO camps. Fortunately, a few of these sessions were broadcast and eventually appeared on record. More than any earlier example, these recordings show the value of Krupa in generating the kind of excitement Goodman sought in his bands. Tough and Fatool might have been more fluid and certainly were more subtle but Krupa gave Benny what he wanted and never really got from anyone else.

This reuniting of the two did not last because when Benny embarked on a long tour Gene stayed in New York to take up an offer from Tommy Dorsey.

During the next few years Benny continued leading his big band with occasional layoffs for vacations, ill-health or, on one occasion, to permit him to duck out of a contract with MCA with whom he no longer felt at ease. Willard Alexander had left to join the Morris agency and soon Benny was there too.

Musically aware of the changes taking place in jazz, Benny kept bop at arm's length for a while although his band continued to number in its ranks several of the younger men whose talents lay somewhat outside the great tradition of the big bands. Tenor saxophonist Stan Getz was one and he can be heard to good, if brief, effect on *Rattle and Roll* and *Swing Angel* where the influence of Lester Young is clearly audible in his playing. Kai Winding made an appearance in the trombone section, as did Bill Harris before moving on to fame with Woody Herman. For a while, however, Benny appeared less than inspired by his fellow musicians – unlike the brief spell in 1943 when Gene and Jess Stacy pushed him to some of his best performances.

44

In 1947, however, Benny decided he could no longer stand on the sidelines making rude remarks about bop. He had never completely ignored it in the hope that it would go away, as did many of his contemporaries. Charlie Christian had talked of what was happening at Minton's so much that as Kenny Clarke recalled, Benny would go down there to listen and to sit in. 'He was all the rage at the time and we always got a great deal of pleasure when he came in. We used to just convert our style to coincide with his, so Benny played just the things he wanted to play.'

Well, it took more than such an ambivalent attitude to make an impact and in 1947 Benny signed with Capitol Records and with an oddly mixed personnel began recording big band bebop which, almost inevitably, fell between two stools.

Chapter Five

The band Benny formed for his first Capitol recordings was very much the mixture as before with veterans of the earlier bands on hand to ensure things didn't vary too much from what the public expected. Mary Lou Williams was one of the arrangers Benny called upon, along with Tommy Todd.

Throughout 1947 the band's personnel changed but there were still older hands like Lou McGarity around although exactly what they thought of newcomers such as Stan Getz, Tommy Pederson and Zoot Sims is open to speculation. Certainly, Getz caused a few problems as Popsie Randolph (Benny's band boy) recalled in *Hear Me Talkin' To Ya*. Stan was 'a cocky kid, just a cocky little boy. A wise guy.' From all accounts Getz, who was twenty at the time, indulged in relatively mild practical jokes and it could well be that a degree of boredom was the motivation. Given what he was to do in later years, the spell with Goodman must have proved irksome to his burgeoning talent.

Benny's attitude towards bop and its practitioners varied considerably. An early comment suggested they were 'just faking. They're just writing and playing for effect and a lot of it doesn't swing.' During the winter of 1947–8, while on the West Coast, he played a concert for Gene Norman and found his views shifting thanks to the musicians with whom he worked. These included Ernie Royal and Wardell Gray of whom Benny clearly approved. 'If Wardell Gray plays bop then it's great because he's wonderful.' Benny also met and approved of Scandinavian clarinetist Stan Hasselgaard and during the early months of 1948 they played together extensively, the only time in his career when Benny fully shared the spotlight with another clarinet player. Broadcasts of the period display a marked similarity between the two musicians, making solo identification extremely difficult.

Wardell Gray also became a fixture with Benny's Sextet which for a time in 1948 was his only regular group, the full orchestra having been temporarily disbanded. When Fats Navarro was added to the Sextet for some Capitol dates it began to look as though Benny was fully won over even if, stylistically, he was still doing what Kenny Clarke had observed during his visits to Minton's and playing in his own way.

Despite Benny's delight in the playing of Gray and Hasselgaard, the younger musicians were not standing still. While airshots and studio recordings of the period show Benny enjoying himself, the fact that he is on an increasingly different musical wavelength is uncomfortably apparent. Gray in particular can be heard maturing session by session. His light tone and highly personal style, apart from being very attractive, help point up one of the essential problems confronting an adventurous musician compelled to play within the relatively rigid and occasionally overpowering confines of a big band.

Stan Hasselgaard might well have become one of the very few clarinet players to move successfully into bop but, sadly, he was killed in a road accident in November 1948 before he was fully into his stride.

Lee Konitz was another of the young guard who floated around the edges of Benny's bebop band. The saxophonist had been prompted to take up music and the clarinet by hearing records of Benny Goodman. At the time Konitz was only eleven years old but by now his musical ideas had changed and although he rehearsed with the band he didn't join. 'Benny wasn't too cool,' he remarked. 'In fact, he was outright corny to me.'

In mid-1948 Benny took an acting role in a movie. This was a remake of the Gary Cooper–Barbara Stanwyck comedy *Ball of Fire* (which had featured Gene Krupa's band) but made the grave error of casting Danny Kaye and Virginia Mayo in the leading roles. Benny spoke his lines, played some classical clarinet, and was 'taught' how to play jazz. Louis Armstrong, Lionel Hampton and Benny

Carter were among several dozen musicians wasted in the film. In any event, acting offers certainly did not flood to Benny's door from Hollywood.

Late in 1948 another bop band was formed, this time without any of the old guard being present. Wardell Gray remained and Doug Mettome who had replaced the unreliable Fats Navarro in the earlier small group, was in the trumpet section. The trombones included Eddie Bert and Milt Bernhart already known for their work with Stan Kenton. Chico O'Farrill's arrangements were good but once again the end result was often unsatisfactory. There were simply too many men playing too many notes and the talents within the sections only rarely had opportunities to stretch. Among recorded exceptions were *Undercurrent Blues* and *Egg Head* which managed to strike almost the right balance.

On *Undercurrent Blues* the sections are tight without being stiff and Eddie Bert solos well. Solo honours, however, go to Doug Mettome whose brilliant trumpet sparks the whole piece. The tension drops noticeably when Benny solos and he sounds ill-at-ease. On *Egg Head*, recorded eight months later, Wardell Gray plays with what was rapidly becoming his elegant ease. Benny makes even fewer concessions to the idiom than usual and while his solo is good if heard out of context, in the piece as a whole it is simply unsuitable.

The small group tracks of the period are better. *Bedlam* by the Septet has good work from Gray and Mettome (here less extrovert than on *Undercurrent Blues*) and on *Blue Lou*. Benny, however, is unhappy and the rhythm section is also caught between two styles. The ensemble passages on *Bedlam* and *Blue Lou* are frankly scrappy and the precision with which Benny Goodman was always associated is absent.

It couldn't last, of course, because Benny was always acutely aware of how he sounded. Inevitably, in a bebop context, he could never be Number One and being second-best was simply not good enough. Before long, therefore, the flirtation with bop ended with Benny remarking that he had never really liked it. As Chico O'Farrill put it, Benny 'realised that, harmonically speaking, bop wasn't his idiom.' Certainly, he never made any serious concessions in his own playing and the big band, saddled as it was with incompatible musicians, never fully came to grips with the new arrangements of all the old tunes. In any event, the big band format was not suited to bop and, an unstated but doubtless pertinent factor, bop was not especially good for business and Benny was always a businessman.

He now formed a small group but a planned tour of Europe hit snags when the Musicians Union in Britain dug in its heels and refused permission for the Septet to play any of its proposed dates. The deal permitted was for Benny to play the London Palladium as a solo while his pianist of the time, Buddy Greco, was allowed in too because he also sang. Benny played two weeks at the Palladium backed by the Skyrockets. The tour of the rest of Europe also failed to come off, this time as a result of problems with currency restrictions.

Back in the States, Benny finally broke up the bebop big band around October and while of itself that fact probably did not upset too many people it did have one lasting sad note – this was the last permanent big band to bear the name of Benny Goodman. From here on his big bands would be specially assembled for tours overseas or for TV spectaculars and the like.

Benny took a quartet on a tour of the Philippines during the winter of 1949–50 and small groups would continue to be formed at regular intervals but as the 1950s began Benny was entering a new phase of his career. Among other things, now, more than ever before, his long-held interest in classical music was allowed much freer rein.

Chapter Six

Benny's interest in the classics dated from his early training with Franz Schoepp at Chicago's Hull-House. The pieces he played for Schoepp were classical and if his working life through the late 1920s and most of the 1930s did not permit much attention he never completely ignored these other areas of music.

Late in 1935 he played the Mozart Clarinet Quintet, K581, at a house party at the home of John Hammond's mother, an occasion which Hammond recalls as being the first time Benny had played a classical piece before an audience. In 1937 Benny recorded with the Pro Arte String Quartet with less than satisfactory results. Similarly unsatisfactory was a recording of the Mozart with the Budapest String Quartet. Given Benny's perfectionism such performances were bound to rankle and he continued to practise his classical playing. As Hammond points out this was something which necessarily affected his playing of all other musical forms since the techniques of classical playing are different in certain important respects. The change to the A clarinet instead of the B-flat instrument was not of itself especially significant but the change of embouchure was. This change (to holding the mouthpiece in the lips instead of between top lip and bottom teeth) altered the sound of his playing, creating as it did a notable absence of vibrato. It also helped develop his distinctive tone which in turn influenced other musicians in jazz for whom tone had not previously held such an important place.

As Benny persisted with his classical practising other performances resulted, in both recording studio and concert hall, which gradually gained him respect and admiration among classicists. On 6 January, 1939, he played Carnegie Hall with Josef Szigeti and Béla Bartók, performing a work he had commissioned from Bartók. This was *Contrasts* for Violin, Clarinet and Piano and in May the following year the same trio recorded the work.

Other concert performances included the Mozart Clarinet Concerto with the Buffalo Philharmonic in November, 1939 and Debussy's First Rhapsody for Clarinet and the Mozart at Carnegie Hall in December, 1940 where he was with the Philharmonic Symphony Orchestra of New York under the baton of John Barbirolli. During the 1940s the trend continued with classical performances not only interspersed with jazz dates but sometimes at mixed concerts. Another commissioned work, Alex North's *Revue for Clarinet and Orchestra*, was performed with the NBC Symphony Orchestra under Leonard Bernstein, this at a time when Benny was beginning to think about the bebop band. Small wonder then, that with his style of playing so firmly rooted in the Swing Era he had helped launch, and with his sound and current inclinations dominated by the classics, that he never fully came to grips with bop.

Indeed, listening to the recordings he made for Capitol during the late 1940s, the only times he sounds fully at ease are on some Trio dates on which he was joined by Teddy Wilson and the former Jimmie Lunceford drummer, Jimmy Crawford. It must be conceded, however, that these tracks, efficient though they are, sound uninspired when set against the earlier Trio's versions.

In the winter months, 1949–50, with the big band folded for ever, Benny spread his interests equally between jazz and the classics and spent some time studying with Reginald Kell. His interest in the classics had, of course, extended to his daughter Rachel who was studying piano.

For Benny, the coming decades were being set and, indeed, with little variation he would spend the next thirty-five years in much the same way.

In April and May of 1950 the postponed European tour took place with Benny bringing a small group to England, later moving on to Sweden. This band included Zoot Sims and Roy Eldridge. Back in the States later the same year he was featured on many TV shows once again with a small group which included vibraphone-player

Terry Gibbs and Teddy Wilson. This and similar groups were also recorded commercially with Benny now back with Columbia records. He also recorded Aaron Copeland's Concerto for Clarinet and Orchestra with the NBC Symphony under Fritz Reiner for the State Department's Voice of America broadcasts. Later the same month, November, he made a commercial recording of the work with the composer conducting the Columbia String Orchestra.

In 1951 Benny immediately agreed to a request from deejay Martin Block to appear at a concert aimed at raising funds for Fletcher Henderson who had suffered severe strokes during the winter. Originally issued as a 'limited edition', the concert subsequently appeared on ordinary commercial records. Opening with a reunited Trio (with Wilson and Krupa) Benny plays as well, if not better than he had during any of the previous five years. After three numbers other musicians joined in one by one until a Septet was onstage. With an old hand like Lou McGarity present and with a trumpet player of the calibre of Buck Clayton around, the session could hardly help but turn out well and it must have warmed the hearts of many of Benny's fans who had quailed at the sounds of the bebop band.

Regular TV and some radio work followed with Benny mostly fronting a Sextet but one date, in January, 1953, brought the old Trio together for an NBC TV date. This was just a few days after Fletcher Henderson's death on 24 December, 1952, and in February 1953 Benny formed a big band for a record date to memorialise Henderson. Using Henderson arrangements on such tunes as *Wolverine Blues* and *What a Little Moonlight Can Do* this band sounded well without ever quite capturing the spirit of the earlier days.

It was around this time that the Carnegie Hall concert recordings were released. The enormous acclaim with which they were greeted prompted Benny to consider bringing together the old gang and taking a big band on the road for a nationwide tour. Teddy Wilson and Gene Krupa were approached and accepted and soon others were signing up. True, some alternatives had to be found but they were mostly of a standard at least as high as that of the men in whose chairs they sat. The eventual line up was: Charlie Shavers, Ziggy Elman, Al Stewart (t); Vernon Brown, Rex Peer (tb); Clint Neagley, Willie Smith (as); Georgie Auld, Sol Schlinger (a classical musician) (ts); Wilson, Steve Jordan (g), Israel Crosby (b) and Krupa. Helen

Ward was brought in as vocalist and rehearsals began. Unfortunately, Benny then began to have second thoughts and as a precaution against failure he proposed adding Louis Armstrong and his All Stars to the bill.

After an out-of-town tryout the band and 'added attraction' came into New York. Precisely what happened next is still clouded, with even Russ Connor and John Hammond (who was involved in the tour's promotion) being unable to cast light on it all.

Somewhere along the way Benny clearly had third thoughts, deciding now that the tour would be successful without Louis who was, anyway, hamming it up with his gallery-raising performance and occasional lapses into material best suited to vaudeville. But, how could Benny remove Louis from the bill? He couldn't fire him; he could, perhaps, have asked him to leave but confronting Louis Armstrong was somewhat different to turning the Goodman 'ray' on a recalcitrant sideman.

There was one other way. After Carnegie Hall performances, at which Benny was decidedly below par (although the press was ecstatic), he was suddenly hospitalized and rumours flew. Various illnesses were reported and in some cases he was said to have died. The tour went on with Louis emceeing and Gene leading Benny's band. Eventually, when the tour was over and the dust had settled, Benny reappeared, now fit and well.

Through the rest of 1953 and 1954 Benny played TV dates, sometimes with Teddy and Gene, and led a Sextet at such varied establishments as New York's Basin Street, the Frontier Hotel in Las Vegas, and at the Hollywood Bowl. He even appeared on Ed Murrow's TV show, 'Person to Person', in which cameras were allowed to invade the usually guarded privacy of his Connecticut home. Early in 1955 he also played Carnegie Hall for a classical concert where he guested with the New York Philharmonic.

A specially assembled small group made some good recordings, mostly of old standards, in March. Benny was accompanied by Teddy Wilson, Perry Lopez (g), Milt Hinton (b) and Bobby Donaldson (d), the group being expanded on some titles by the addition of Ruby Braff (cnt), Urbie Green (tb) and Paul Quinichette (ts). Perhaps it was the revival of interest in his music, but Benny was certainly on form in *After You've Gone, Body and Soul, Memories of You* and others.

The band was formed to play a regular weekend engagement at New York's Basin Street in the spring of 1955. The issued recordings were made at the club about half-way through the residency, which lasted ten weekends, and the band, obviously well-rehearsed, offers a tight ensemble sound with the rhythm section in good swinging form. The other front-line instrumentalists all have extensive solo space and take good advantage of it. Benny's form is good although overfamiliarity with much of the material is occasionally apparent.

In July he headed west to Hollywood to be on hand while *The Benny Goodman Story* was filmed. For all its accuracy, both musically and in terms of its storyline, he might just as well have stayed at home.

The band assembled for the film mixed some of the old gang with some interlopers and, judging from the resulting performances, not a few of Universal's studio musicians were on hand too. Of the biggest stars of the old band, Gene Krupa was there as were Teddy Wilson and Lionel Hampton (acting in a travesty of the scene in which he is 'discovered' by Benny) but Harry James turns up only in the closing sequences when the band runs through *Sing, Sing, Sing* in a simulation of the 1938 Carnegie Hall concert. Reputedly, Harry was wanted for more than this token appearance but at a conference during pre-production Benny was asked how much Harry should be paid. 'Pay him what he was paid the last time we worked together,' he said. As they hadn't worked together for almost fifteen years there is little wonder that Harry found more pressing demands on his time.

Harry James was far from being the only musician to fall foul of Benny's care with money. Red Rodney has recalled an occasion when he played with Goodman and found himself graduated to lead trumpet as other men left and, naturally enough, suggested a raise was in order. He was fired. Richie Kamuca, one time down on his luck, had a call from Benny suggesting lunch. Richie agreed eagerly. Surely this meant a job was in the offing, and, given that he had not been eating too well, lunch itself would be a real treat. He met Benny at a classy New York restaurant, they talked and Richie ate. And ate. Then Benny told him how much he had enjoyed the meeting, stood up and left. No job had been offered, and, worse, Benny had not paid the bill.

Jess Stacy was also absent from the Hollywood version of Benny's life. Not unreasonably given his long service with Goodman, he had asked to be given a speaking part but was refused. John Hammond was in, then out, and at one point threatened legal action but eventually was 'in' through the appearance of an actor in his role (which was drastically truncated as the part he played in Benny's real-life story did not suit what the scriptwriters thought should have happened). Steve Allen, a chat-show host, actor and approximate musician, played the part of Benny Goodman. Benny, of course, played on the soundtrack but all things considered, Hollywood did what it usually does on such occasions and made a mess of what could have been an interesting musical and social document which brought together so many strands in American life and dreams.

The movie over, Benny continued recording with small groups and occasionally even a big band, in one instance remaking much of the music from the movie in an attempt to do it better this time. Certainly, the results had a better sound as the recordings made at Universal have a dull, muffled quality but even so the fire is missing.

The release of the film in February 1956 prompted the reforming of a big band for an engagement at New York's Waldorf-Astoria followed by a short tour.

Benny was just as much interested in recording classical pieces as anything else and this year saw recordings of performances at Tanglewood of the Mozart Clarinet Concerto in A and the Mozart Quintet.

At the end of the year, the State Department came up with a suggestion that held immediate appeal for Benny. This was to take a band on a goodwill tour of the Far East. The band played Japan, already beginning the enormous shift towards jazz which would eventually make it a home from home for many visiting Americans, and then moved on to Thailand where Benny met and played duets with Phumiphol Aduljej, a real king. The king even joined in a radio broadcast on which he played soprano saxophone in a Sextet version of *On the Sunny Side of the Street.*

The tour continued to Burma before heading back to the States and an appearance for Benny, and a somewhat modified band, on the Ed Sullivan show. This band made a short tour before being wound up. Benny played several TV dates usually with small groups assembled especially, while a big band, labelled as The Benny Goodman Orchestra, toured across the nation under the leadership of Urbie Green.

Another overseas tour was suggested by the State Department, this time to Europe, and in May 1958 Benny headed for Berlin with a band including Taft Jordan (t) and Zoot Sims in its ranks. With Benny's dubious approval, singer Jimmy Rushing was also included. After Berlin this band played the Concertgebouw in Amsterdam before moving on to Brussels for the World's Fair. Some of the performances at the Fair were recorded and there is certainly more zest to this band than to many of the 'specials'. No small credit for this goes to Jimmy Rushing whose infectious enthusiasm and powerful, swinging style lifted the band. All Benny's doubts about Mr Five by Five were proved unjustified and the band and Benny clearly enjoyed themselves. Equally clearly, audiences loved it all too.

Back in the States Benny played the Newport Jazz Festival with a similar band; some changes took out Zoot Sims (replaced by Buddy Tate) and brought in Billy Butterfield (t). The band's drummer remained and stayed around for quite a while. Either Benny was mellowing in his distaste for many of the drummers with whom he worked over the years or maybe, in Roy Burnes, he had finally found one who suited him.

1959 was much as the previous year had been. TV shows, club engagements, all with small groups from Trio up to Octet and there was even time for a holiday in London. Then another overseas tour was set up covering one North African and five European countries. Twenty cities in three weeks must have been hard work but the band and Benny were in good form. With musicians of the calibre of Bill Harris, Flip Phillips and Red Norvo around, to say nothing of Jack Sheldon there to keep up everyone's spirits, this was an exceptional tour which was fortunately recorded for radio broadcasting in various countries. The vocalist on this tour was Anita O'Day whose talents had now become apparent even to Benny.

A spirit of enthusiasm abounds and Benny is clearly booted along by his companions. Everyone is allocated plenty of solo space and the concerts were varied in structure to take advantage of all possible variations of small groups from within the group's ranks. For the maestro's numerous European fans, this tour provided many vintage moments.

At the end of the decade, Benny made a TV appearance for CBS in New York which reunited him with Gene and Lionel and Jess Stacy. The change of pianist in what is otherwise the original Quartet makes a notable difference. On up-tempo numbers like *Avalon* and *I Got Rhythm* Stacy's style is chunkier than ears accustomed to Teddy Wilson's fleet playing expect and, perhaps surprisingly, it suits the other musicians very well. On ballads like *Where Or When* there is an added texture absent in many performances by the original four. Stacy had of course played in small groups drawn from the big band before Wilson came along to be specially featured and these later recordings provide an interesting hint as to how the small groups might have developed in other hands. In some respects Stacy bring an earthier sound but it appears likely that this would not have resulted in the instant broad appeal to which Wilson made an inimitable contribution.

The 1960s began much as the 1950s had ended, with TV shows and various club dates and radio transmissions. At a party given by the Governor of New York, Benny was reunited with the King of Thailand during an impromptu jam session at which the real king demonstrated his ability on other reed instruments by forsaking his soprano for an alto saxophone.

Various tours were proposed with Canada coming off while Britain yet again tangled itself up in wrangles with the MU and was eventually cancelled. At the end of 1961 Benny made a three-week tour of South America with a big band. Then, in March 1962 a tour was announced which ensured front page coverage for Benny. This was to Russia.

Before he left for Moscow, however, Benny played another prestigious gig, one calculated to ensure he would not be seduced by communism: the White House, where his audience included President Kennedy and British Prime Minister Harold Macmillan.

Before departure Benny also played Seattle's World's Fair and various other dates, finally leaving New York on 27 May. The band opened the tour at Moscow's Sports Palace on 30 May (Benny's 53rd birthday) and another world leader came to listen: Premier Nikita Khrushchev. After various dates in the Soviet Union, which were greeted ecstatically by the crowds, they returned to Moscow where, on 4 July Benny attended a function at the US Embassy and found himself arguing the relative merits of jazz and other musical forms with the Premier who was not well-pleased with the adulation lavished upon the American visitor.

Various tours and engagements followed Benny's return to the

States and in January, 1963, he was featured on an NBC TV show, 'The World Of Benny Goodman'. This showed film clips from the tours of Russia, the Far East and Europe among other snippets from Benny's screen appearances.

Benny continued to make classical recordings and broadcasts but for the hardcore fan the recording sessions of February and August, 1963 were what they had been waiting for. The resulting album was entitled 'Together Again' and it featured the original Quartet.

With everyone on good form (if anything, Benny was marginally overshadowed by Teddy, Lionel and Gene) the resulting run through of all the old favourites, and some different tunes was a delight but adds little, except recording quality, to what had been done in the past. Despite, or perhaps because of, familiarity the musicians are more at ease on tunes like *Runnin' Wild* and *Seven Come Eleven* than on, say *Who Cares?* and *Dearest.*

Early in 1964 Benny toured Japan, where he was greeted enthusiastically, with a less notable quartet. But Dick Shreve (p) and Colin Bailey (d) acquitted themselves well while the bass player, Monty Budwig, showed clear evidence of his standing as one of the most formidable of the new generation of jazz musicians.

Back in the States Benny played a benefit concert with his daughter Rachel. Among other works they performed the Brahms Sonata for Clarinet and Piano, No. 1.

A mixture of jazz concerts and classical recitals followed through the year while in August in New York the 22nd was designated 'Benny Goodman Day'. In London the following month he played classics (with the Pro Arte Strings) and jazz (with Ronnie Scott and others) on 'Gala Performance' for BBC TV.

The balance of this decade continued in much the same manner: classical recitals, jazz concerts, TV dates and occasional limited tours. There was also a celebratory dinner party on 16 January 1968 at which many of the stalwarts from Carnegie Hall thirty years before were on hand. There were also a few times spent in bed as his old back ailment struck again and again.

A visit to London in 1969 was an opportunity to record with a specially assembled big band of British musicians and Benny was sufficiently impressed to make a Scandinavian tour with a similar group a few months later. At no time does this band sound like a 'Benny Goodman band' but the high quality of arrangements and playing make this one of his most satisfactory associations of the past decade.

Nevertheless, given that the end of the 1960s brought him to the end of his 43rd year as a recording artist and similarly chalked up his 47th year as a professional musician, he was in remarkably good form. Of course, despite those figures, he was still only sixty years old and, given his present way of working – interspersing performing with time off to relax – he could confidently expect to continue an active career into the 1970s and beyond.

Chapter Seven

For the fans, perhaps the most entertaining aspects of Benny Goodman's work in the early 1970s were the regular regroupings of the original Quartet. Of course, Lionel Hampton was engaged with his own big band of up-and-coming youngsters (Lionel's bands were *always* filled with such future stars); Teddy Wilson was working steadily as a solo, and Gene Krupa was gravely ill, but they all seemed to find the time for these get-togethers.

A New York TV show in 1972 (Gene's health prevented them from working far afield), produced cracking performances of *Avalon, Moonglow* and *I'm a Ding Dong Daddy* that lacked none of the old fire.

In 1973 Benny celebrated his 64th birthday at a party at New York's Rainbow Grill (delayed a day as his back ailment had flared up causing him to spend 30 May in bed). He was appearing at this time with a small group including Bobby Hackett (t), Milt Hinton (b), John Bunch (p) and the British-born vibraphone-player Pete Appleyard. Lionel Hampton came along to sit in and quite clearly Benny was enjoying life. As he remarked to John S. Wilson of *The New York Times,* he was doing what he wanted to do and had no intention of retiring. 'You can't turn the switch off and say you're finished. I love to play.'

Also in 1973, the Quartet, filled out with bass-player Slam Stewart, played Carnegie Hall. Even though, by this time, Krupa was visibly ailing the four-plus-one swung mightily. Teddy Wilson was in excellent form and extended himself on *C-Jam Blues* while everyone else was featured on the old familiar favourites: *How High the Moon* for Lionel, *Sing, Sing, Sing* for Gene and, appropriately enough, for Benny a superb *Memories of You*. Even Slam Stewart's highly personal style was brought to bear on a standard from the Quartet's early days, *Oh! Lady Be Good*.

The day before the concert, 29 June, the five men had gathered for an extended rehearsal and, as Tom Buckley of *The New York Times* reported, this was primarily to confirm that Gene could stand the strain. As the drummer remarked to the reporter, he was suffering from leukaemia and required regular blood transfusions. Somewhat optimistically, he added that as the disease was in a benign form he hoped to continue playing for some time yet. Certainly, recordings of the concert on 30 June show no sign that Krupa was rapidly approaching the end of his life.

This Carnegie Hall appearance was a part of the Newport Jazz Festival and festivals had now become a regular part of Benny's working life. 1973 also saw him in New Orleans for the Jazz and Heritage Festival. Similar performances continued into 1974 but there were no more appearances by the original Quartet as Gene Krupa had died in October, 1973. At the Schaefer Music Festival, held in New York's Central Park in June, Benny started out with a Sextet but the enthusiasm of both audience and musicians swelled the ranks. A pair of elderly jitterbugs came out of retirement and reprised the Paramount Theatre scenes of more than a quarter-century before by dancing in the aisles. To everyone's surprise the jeaned and sneakered younger generation watched this display only briefly before joining in. The band dug in, Benny clearly had a whale of a time, and soon found himself leading a nine-piece group, including veteran Chris Griffin and stalwarts of middle-period Goodman bands such as Urbie Green and Slam Stewart.

Towards the end of 1974 Benny flew to London for an appearance at the Royal Albert Hall where the band included Stewart, Bucky Pizarelli (g), Hank Jones (p) and another Chris Griffin, this one playing drums. As Marjorie Traill reported for *Jazz Journal*, Benny's tone was as satin-like as ever and even if the years had left their mark 'by this showing there is no doubt he is still a major jazz clarinetist.'

Through 1975 Benny continued his playing career mixing benefits, such as one for the music division of the New York Public

61

Library at which he performed with operatic baritone Sherrill Milnes and Boston Pops conductor Arthur Fiedler, with more adventurous forays which took in concerts in California, New Hampshire and even north to Alaska. As he remarked to *The NYT's* John S. Wilson, he was 'doing better business now than . . . in the Swing Era.'

During one 1975 concert, again at the annual Schaefer Music Festival, this time in a heat-wave, a very-much on-form Zoot Sims pushed Benny into one of his best performances of recent times. At one point, presumably overtaken by a severe case of nostalgia, Benny harked back to his musical beginnings, dropped to one knee and revived his old Ted Lewis impersonation.

Also in 1975, Benny recorded several sessions which resulted from an appearance in TV's 'The World of John Hammond'. Benny met up with one of the new generation of guitarists, George Benson, and one of the oldest jazzmen around, Joe Venuti. With Benson, Benny found a surprising rapport although the record date failed to capture the magic of their TV meeting. With Joe Venuti, then in full cry during the resurgence in his career (which had begun around the same time as Benny's), Benny had a ball. Backed by a sound rhythm section and also joined by Al Grey and Urbie Green, these recordings of late 1975 found Benny in excellent form. Nevertheless, most of his time was spent relaxing at home with his festival and concert appearances serving simply to fulfil his music-making needs. Quite clearly, he did not need the money.

But then, in 1978, Alice Goodman died and Benny's work now developed another purpose as he needed to occupy time he would otherwise have spent at home. Benny's private life had always remained precisely that – private. His Connecticut home was off-limits to all but a few close friends. That momentary lapse in 1954, when he had allowed TV cameras in, was never repeated. The children, Rachel apart, did not enter public life although, along with Rachel, some of his and Alice's daughters did have tunes named after them (*Rachel's Dream*, *Gilly*, *Hi 'Ya Sophia*, *Benjie's Bubble*). Now, without Alice, Benny's private life, so jealously guarded, was empty.

He continued working and touring, covering America, Europe and the Far East. In September 1980 he played the Aurex Jazz Festival held at Tokyo, Yokohama and Osaka with a group including Teddy Wilson. For the most part they played the old standards and the rest of the band: Tony Terran (t), Dick Nash (tb), Eddie Duran (g), Al Obidenski (b) and John Markham (d) did what was required of them but Benny's sparkling form obviously owed much to Teddy Wilson. The pianist excelled himself (not just with Benny but in sessions with Benny Carter and others at the festival), playing in a powerful, romping manner which emphatically answered back those of his critics who regard much of his work as effete.

In October 1981 Benny was at Snape Maltings, Aldeburgh, England for a week of classical performances with the Amadeus String Quartet. On this same occasion he joined pianist Clifford Curzon with whom he played Brahms. The week was rounded out with a jazz concert at which he was accompanied by violinist Svend Asmussen and very ably backed by a British rhythm section: Brian Lemon (p), Phil Lee (g), Lennie Bush (b) and Martin Drew (d).

Benny sounded very relaxed on tunes like *So Easy to Remember, Don't Be That Way, Stompin' at the Savoy* and *Memories of You*. At one point in the evening, Benny declared that 'there's a great *simpatico* between Svend and myself, so we'd like to play quite a few songs with just the violin and the clarinet.' And so they did, with a particularly delightful reading of *If I Had You* and an intelligent improvisation on *After You've Gone* which, while never straying far from the melody, was taken at a mercifully easy tempo instead of the tear-up rate of so many of the small group performances.

In real terms, however, there was no new ground to be broken – not that this is offered as an adverse comment. Quite clearly, Benny had long since done all that he could in giving to American popular music one of its most significant chapter headings.

Chapter Eight

Following Benny Goodman's death on 13 June 1986 the Swing Era, by then more than half a century old, was finally laid to rest. Any history of jazz carries an obligatory passage on the Swing Era but sometimes there is a curious attempt to downplay Benny Goodman's importance. It is this unwillingness on the part of some writers to acknowledge Benny's place in jazz that most irritates his fans. The key to the reason for the occasional damning with faint praise lies, of course, in his enormous commercial success. For a jazzman to become a millionaire is somehow regarded as a sure sign of a sell-out. That many jazz musicians made money and lost it (either through sheer extravagance or, all too often, through the stupidity or criminality of their advisers) is oddly acceptable. To make money and keep it, something which any hard-headed businessman would be proud to achieve, is considered incompatible with artistic integrity. In the case of jazz the waters are forever muddied by the successes of white musicians of the 1930s who, led by Benny Goodman, popularised music that was initially the preserve of black Americans.

This is no place to argue this point but while there have been countless examples of inferior white bands making money while superior black bands foundered, this should not be used to justify criticism of Goodman.

In his early years, playing in and around his home town of Chicago, Benny was assiduous in his pursuit of jazz whether to play or to listen to. He was also determined to make his playing as perfect

Benny Goodman at the Savoy Hotel, London, 1959.
Photo: Central Press Photos Ltd.

left: *John Hammond with French jazz critic Hugues Panassié in 1935.* Photo: Max Jones files

below: *Benny Goodman and his Orchestra, Congress Hotel, Chicago, 1935.* Photo: Frank Driggs Collection. (l to r) Jess Stacy (p), Harry Goodman (b), Allan Reuss (g), Helen Ward (voc), Gene Krupa (d), Benny Goodman (cl), Dick Clark (ts), Harry Geller (t), Bill De Pew (as, bars), Ralph Muzzillo (t), Joe Harris (tb, voc), Nate Kazebier (t), Hymie Schertzer (as), Red Ballard (tb), Art Rollini (ts).

above: *Benny Goodman Trio, c 1937.* (l to r) Benny Goodman, Teddy Wilson, Gene Krupa. Photo: Frank Driggs Collection

below: *Benny Goodman Quartet, 1937.* (l to r) Lionel Hampton, Teddy Wilson, Benny Goodman, Gene Krupa. Photo: Frank Driggs Collection.

left: *Benny Goodman and Gene Krupa, 1938.* Photo: Max Jones files

above: *The Benny Goodman Orchestra during a Camel Caravan Broadcast, New York, 1939.* Photo: Frank Driggs Collection. (l to r) Jess Stacy (p), George Rose (g), Nick Fatool (d), Artie Bernstein (b), Jerry Jerome (ts), Red Ballard (tb), Ziggy Elman (t), Hymie Schertzer (as), Corky Cornelius (t), Vernon Brown (tb), Toots Mondello (as), Chris Griffin (t), Benny Goodman (cl), Bus Bassey (ts).

above: *Benny Goodman Sextet, 1941.* (l to r) Georgie Auld (ts), Benny Goodman (cl), Charlie Christian (g), Artie Bernstein (b), Cootie Williams (t). Not visible: Johnny Guarnieri (p), Dave Tough (d). Photo: Frank Driggs Collection.

below: *"Swingin' the Dream", Center Threatre, New York, 1939.* (l to r) Fletcher Henderson (p), Charlie Christian (g), Nick Fatool (d), Lionel Hampton (vibs), Artie Bernstein (b), Benny Goodman (cl). Photo: Frank Driggs Collection.

above: *The Benny Goodman Orchestra in "Stage Door Canteen", 1942.* (l to r)
Irving Goodman (t), Charlie Castaldo (tb), Jess Stacy (p), Miff Mole (tb),
Hal Peppie (t), Joe Rushton (bss), Lee Castle (t), Louis Bellson (d), Peggy
Lee (voc), unknown (ts), ?Cliff Hill (b), Benny Goodman (cl), ?Clint
Neagley (as), John Walton (ts). Photo: Frank Driggs Collection.

below: *Benny Goodman and his Orchestra appearing with Marian McPartland
on Johnny Carson's Tonight Show.* Photo: Max Jones files.

above: *Benny Goodman, with (l to r) Teddy Wilson, Lionel Hampton, Slam Stewart and Gene Krupa, participating in the 1973 Newport Jazz Festival at Carnegie Hall, New York.* Photo: David Redfern.

below: *Bucky Pizzarelli, Zoot Sims, Benny Goodman and Pete Appleyard in concert, 1972.* Photo: Jan Persson.

Benny Goodman. Photo: David Redfern.

as possible and the measure of his success is that he became the first clarinet virtuoso in jazz (and there have been precious few in his wake). Virtuoso ability is not, of course, a prerequisite of jazz (were it so, many of the most important innovators and practitioners would have fallen by the wayside) but at his jazz best Benny seldom allowed preoccupation with technique to get in the way of a satisfactorily hot performance.

There can be little doubt that the change in embouchure did cause some difficulties in permitting him to play in a manner which suited the critics. Yet, in performances set as wide apart in time as the Hotsy Totsy Gang in 1929, the USO band of 1943 and the British band he led on a European tour in 1970, he could turn in powerful, hot solos for which no apologies are needed.

His big bands over the years have certainly shown a heavy dependence upon skilled and compatible arrangers. Few could doubt that the band of the Palomar, the Paramount, the Congress and the Madhattan Room would never have attained its success and popularity without Jimmy Mundy's and Fletcher Henderson's charts. Similarly beneficial were the later arrangements written by Mel Powell and Eddie Sauter and, even if it never quite got off the ground, the bebop band's charts by Chico O'Farrill made the very best of infertile ground. In his dependence upon skilled arrangers for the big band Goodman was no different to most other bands, black and white, of similar periods. Don Redman, Edgar Sampson for Chick Webb, George Handy for Boyd Raeburn, all provided similar help. Only Ellington and Basie were different in this respect, tending to rely upon collective and/or improvisational arranging — but, then, comparisons with Basie are bound to prove detrimental whether writing of Goodman or almost anyone else.

Benny's compositions are few and, indeed, many of those pieces which bear his name list him only co-composer. Of these, however much he might have been responsible for popularising them, most are essentially the work of others.

Benny's status in the eyes of other musicians has usually been high when tested in musical terms if somewhat guarded on a personal level. Even those who fell victim to his whims or were fried by over-exposure to the Goodman 'ray' never put him down as a performer.

It is in his small group work where Benny's abilities as a jazzman are most readily apparent. With the Trio and the Quartet he proved time and time again that whether playing lyrically on a ballad or digging into a swinging performance on one or another of the old flagwavers he could, and regularly did, play as well as any contemporary clarinetist without regard for colour or background.

In the Quartet and Trio Benny also introduced another element which cannot be overlooked, the hiring of black musicians to work on-stage with whites. True, he had to be persuaded by John Hammond that the first of these moves, asking Teddy Wilson to join, was not a way to financial disaster; but, once the move was made, he persisted through the hiring of Lionel Hampton and on to Charlie Christian, Cootie Williams, Big Sid Catlett and beyond. Clearly Goodman was not alone but he was certainly the first to establish high-profile integration. Given his national fame, no one could suggest he was sneaking black musicians on-stage without general public awareness.

In terms of helping the careers of musicians who might otherwise have languished on the sidelines, Goodman's role becomes a little more problematical. Some of the routinely average sidemen he worked with in the 1930s and early 1940s probably made a better living than they really deserved. Others, like Krupa and Harry James, went on to great success with the boost their time in the Goodman band provided. It can be supposed that both Teddy Wilson and Lionel Hampton would have continued their already upward careers without Goodman; but perhaps Wilson's would have been a long, slow haul although Lionel's exuberance and propensity towards flash and spectacle would have ensured his success anyway. Whether it would have come when it did, or with the same measure of world-wide recognition without Goodman is another matter. Additionally, Benny gaves James, Wilson and Hampton financial help.

In the case of Charlie Christian, without Goodman's acceptance of him, and, of course, John Hammond's persistence, who can tell if the skinny kid with no dress sense and the unfashionable electric guitar would not have stayed in Oklahoma City and obscurity. If Benny Goodman had done nothing else for jazz, his role in the life and career, short as it tragically was, of Charlie Christian would ensure him an honoured place in all histories.

But Benny did do much else, however unwittingly. He made jazz over into a form accessible to and acceptable by a large slice of the white middle-class in America. If there had been no Swing Era, jazz today would be just as rich in musical terms. What the Era achieved was a widening of public appeal and if this diluted jazz, it also helped to make it financially viable.

Of course, Benny became rich; but if he made a good living out of jazz he also ensured that so too did many of his contemporaries and successors, black as well as white, although perhaps not many other wealthy musicians clung onto their money with such determination. It has been suggested, sometimes with malice but usually with wry humour, that Benny kept until the day he died that first $5 bill he earned at the age of twelve for his Ted Lewis impersonation. Yet, given Benny's childhood – the huge family, the paltry income from Pop Goodman's labours at the clothing factory, the lack of adequate food, the needs imposed upon him as the family's best-equipped breadwinner after his father's death – is it surprising that he had a high regard for money?

Now that Goodman is gone and all that remains are the records and tapes of his vast recorded output, his role in the history of jazz and of American popular music will undoubtedly find him to have been a figure of great importance. Never an innovator, often dependent upon others for inspiration, he nevertheless provided a valuable centralising force for many of the best musicians of his and later generations.

In performance he was almost invariably sound and always highly musical. After the earliest recordings his technique tended to conceal the fact that he really was a very good jazz musician indeed. He was not the first, nor will he be the last, musician to develop a technique so skilled that by making the difficult commonplace and the impossible possible he confused critics who thought that his technique was all there was.

Certainly, there are moments in his later career when he sounds lethargic or bored or disinterested (for example, his dreadfully performed showpieces at the 1978 Carnegie Hall 40th Anniversary Concert). Against this there are moments when he sounds inspired: *Sweet Georgia Brown* in Sweden with the British band in 1970; the Quartet reunion at Carnegie Hall in 1973 and the year before on the TV show in New York at both of which he played an excellent version of *I'm a Ding Dong Daddy* and an exquisite *Memories of You* at the former. Most of the things he did in the 1940s and early 1950s have flashes of brilliance often obscured by the problems of compatability with the bebop band. The small group work of these decades is consistently fine and if there is an element of coasting apparent in much of Benny's playing it has to be conceded that Benny coasting is frequently better than lesser players at full stretch.

Back in the 1930s, whether with the small jazz groups or much of the non-commercial work which predated the formation of the first permanent Benny Goodman band, practically everything he did was touched with a quality no other clarinet player achieved over such a long and continuous period of time.

Perhaps, in the 1920s his playing closely resembled that of other clarinetists. Listening to others soloing on recordings of the period, among them Jimmy Noone, Frank Teschemacher and even Pee Wee Russell on a good day, it needs a good ear to always differentiate between them and Benny. But from 1931 onwards the Goodman style becomes steadily more distinctive and, however much imitated, soon became inimitable.

It is, of course, the big band of the 1930s that comes most readily to mind when Benny's name is mentioned. For those who were young then, and for many who look back nostalgically to times before they were born (a feat neither impossible nor uncommon), the name of Benny Goodman will always be synonymous with the Swing Era.

Perhaps Benny could have done more for jazz as a performer had he not become the King of Swing but such thoughts are idly speculative. Like all men he was made up from many things; in his case a significant factor was the driving ambition which lifted him out of the relatively confined world of the jazz musician.

Through his determination to succeed, he became rich and famous. The path he chose was simple enough – he decided to be the best. If, in the process, he also became a distant, apparently unemotional martinet he probably thought the price was worth it. If he knew what people thought of his manner and his eccentricities, he probably didn't care. Making music was the important thing – by deciding on, and achieving, perfection he also made money and gained fame and lasting recognition. In short, he achieved the American Dream.

It is possible to argue persuasively that as a result of his progress towards the pinnacle of success, Benny became less of a jazzman than he had been as a young man. But this unnecessarily constricts the definition of what makes a jazz musician. By all but the narrowest of definitions, Benny was a jazz musician in his heart – if not in his soul. However, setting aside such thoughts, together with all squabbles over what is and what is not jazz, for a dozen years in the 1930s and 1940s Swing was the thing and Benny Goodman was its King.

Bibliography

Anyone choosing to write about Benny Goodman cannot do other than offer grateful thanks, and no small measure of praise, to Russ Connor for his pioneering work. This and other books and articles to which I have referred are as follows:

Books
Connor, D. Russell and Hicks, Warren W.: *B G, on the Record.*
Arlington House, New York, 1970
Freeman, Bud: *If You Know a Better Life.*
Bashall Eaves, Dublin, 1970
Gitler, Ira: *Jazz Masters of the Forties.*   Collier, New York, 1974
Goodman, Benny and Kolodin, Irving: *The Kingdom of Swing.*
Frederick Ungar, New York, 1961
Hammond, John and Townsend, Irving: *John Hammond on Record.* Penguin, London. 1981
Meeker, David: *Jazz in the Movies.* Talisman, London 1981
Shapiro, Nat and Hentoff, Nat: *Hear Me Talkin' to Ya.*
Penguin, London, 1962
Simon, George T.: *The Big Bands.*   Collier, New York, 1974

Articles
Balliett, Whitney: 'Benny Goodman', *The New Yorker*
December 26, 1977
Voce, Steve: 'It Don't Mean a Thing', *Jazz Journal*
28: 1 January, 1975
Voce, Steve: 'It Don't Mean a Thing', *Jazz Journal*
28: 6 June, 1975
Woolley, Stan: 'Bopping With Benny', *Jazz Journal International*
34: 11 November 1981
and various editions of *The New York Times*.

Discography

The immense volume of Benny Goodman's recorded work makes a comprehensive discography impossible here as it would run to several hundred pages. The following selection suggests representative listening for various periods in Benny's long career. Jazz record collectors will be aware of the speed with which albums are deleted from the catalogues of major companies and of the difficulty in obtaining specialist labels. I have made some allowance for this, concentrating upon relatively recent releases. However, as shops specializing in jazz records, both new and second-hand, can often work minor miracles I have included many imports which offer valuable material which is otherwise unavailable. I am grateful for the help of individuals listed elsewhere and also to Russ Connor's pioneering discographical work. Any errors which exist are mine alone. Abbreviations used are as follows: (as) alto saxophone, (b) bass, (bars) baritone saxophone, (bss) bass saxophone, (bgo) bongo drums, (bjo) banjo, (cel) celeste, (co) cello, (cl) clarinet, (c-mel) c-melody saxophone, (cnt) cornet, (d) drums, (dir) director, (fl) flute, (Fr-h) French horn, (g) guitar, (p) piano, (sx) saxophone, (t) trumpet, (tb) trombone, (ts) tenor saxophone, (tu) tuba, (unk) unknown, (vib) vibraphone, (v) violin, (vcl, voc) vocal, (xyl) xylophone.

BRUCE CROWTHER, *London, August 1987*

BEN POLLACK AND HIS CALIFORNIANS

Harry Greenberg, Al Harris, Earl Baker (t), Glenn Miller (tb), Benny Goodman (cl), Gil Rodin (as), Fud Livingston (ts), Vic Briedis (p,cel), Lou Kessler (g), Harry Goodman (tu), Ben Pollack (d, vcl), The Williams Sisters (vcl).

Chicago, December 17, 1926

| BVE 37219-6 | 'DEED I DO – VOC BP | RCA B&W FXM 1 7283 |
| BVE 37261-3 | HE'S THE LAST WORD – VOC TWS | Sunbeam SB 136 |

BENNY GOODMAN
Benny Goodman (cl), Mel Stitzel (p), Bob Conselman (d).

		Chicago, February, 1927
C 2006	THAT'S A PLENTY	Sunbeam SB 112, Decca RAL508,
		Vocalion VLP 2, Affinity AFS 1018
C 2007	CLARINETITIS	Sunbeam SB 112, Decca RAL508,
		Vocalion VLP 2, Affinity AFS 1018

BEN POLLACK AND HIS ORCHESTRA
Jimmy McPartland (cnt), Frank Quantrell (t), Glenn Miller (tb), Benny Goodman (cl, tp), Gil Rodin (as), Larry Binyon (ts), Vic Briedis (p), Dick Morgan (bjo), Harry Goodman (tu), Ben Pollock (d, vcl). *Chicago, December 7, 1927*

BVE 41342-2	WAITIN' FOR KATIE – VOC BP	RCA B&W FXM 1 7283
BVE 41342-3	WAITIN' FOR KATIE – VOC BP	Sunbeam SB 136
BVE 41343-1	MEMPHIS BLUES	Sunbeam SB 136
BVE 41343-2	MEMPHIS BLUES	RCA B&W FXM 1 7283

BENNY GOODMAN'S BOYS
Quantrell, Rodin, Binyon out; Morgan plays (g); Bob Conselman (d, vib) repl. Pollack. *Chicago, January 23, 1928*

C 1652	A JAZZ HOLIDAY	Sunbeam SB 141, Vocalion VLP 2,
		Affinity AFS 1018
C 1654	WOLVERINE BLUES	Sunbeam SB 141, Vocalion VLP 2,
		Decca RAL 508, Affinity AFS 1018

ALL STAR ORCHESTRA
Jimmy McPartland (cnt), Ray Lodwig, Fuzzy Farrar (t), Glenn Miller, Tommy Dorsey (tb), Benny Goodman (cl), Fud Livingston (ts), Max Farley, unk (sx), unk (Fr-h), unk (p), Carl Kress (bjo), Joe Tarto (tu), Chauncey Morehouse (d), Scrappy Lambert (vcl). *NYC, March 21, 1928*

BVE 43385-1	OH, BABY! – VOC SL	Sunbeam SB 112
BVE 43385-2	OH, BABY! – VOC SL	RCA B&W FXM 1 7283

JOHNNY MARVIN
Jimmy McPartland (cnt) or Mannie Klein (t), Benny Goodman (cl, as), Rube Bloom or Frank Banta (p), Eddie Lang (g), Joe Venuti or Matty Malneck (v), Johnny Marvin (vcl). *NYC, April 19, 1928*

BVE 43578-1	ANGEL – VOC JM	Sunbeam SB 112
BVE 43578-3	ANGEL – VOC JM	RCA B&W FXM 1 7238
add unk. (d)		
BVE 43579-3	MY PET – VOC JM	RCA B&W FXM 1 7283, Sunbeam
		SB112

BEN POLLACK AND HIS CALIFORNIANS
as December 7, 1927 except Al Harris (t), Bud Freeman (ts) repl. Quantrell, Binyon, add Ed Bergman, Al Beller (v), unk (cello). *NYC, April 26, 1928*

BVE 43540-4	SINGAPORE SORROWS – VOC BP	Sunbeam SB 136

IRENE BEASLEY
Benny Goodman (cl, as), unk. t, p, g, v, cello.   *NYC, May, 1928*
BVE 43935-2   THE ST. LOUIS BLUES – VOC IB   RCA B&W FXM 1 7283
                                        similar *NYC, May 5, 1928*
BVE 45006-2   CHOO-CHOO TRAIN – VOC IB   RCA B&W FXM 1 7283, Sunbeam
                                                           SB 112

BENNY GOODMAN'S BOYS
as January 23, 1928 except add Fud Livingston (cl, as), Ben Pollack (d) repl.
Conselman. Goodman also plays as, bars, cnt.   *NYC, June 4, 1928*
E27638   JUNGLE BLUES   Sunbeam SB 141, Vocalion VLP2, Affinity
                                                           AFS 1018
E 27638-alt   JUNGLE BLUES   Sunbeam 112
E 27639   ROOM 1411   Sunbeam SB 141, Vocalion VLP2, Decca RAL 508
                                                    Affinity AFS 1018
E 27639-alt   ROOM 1411   Sunbeam 112
E 27640   BLUE   Sunbeam SB 141, Decca RAL 508, Affinity AFS 1018
add Tommy Dorsey (tb)
E 27643   SHIRT TAIL STOMP   Sunbeam SB 141, Vocalion VLP 2, Affinity
                                                           AFS 1018

BEN POLLACK AND HIS PARK CENTRAL ORCHESTRA
as April 26, 1928 except Jack Teagarden (tb) repl. Miller, Bill Schumann (cello)
repl. unk., add Belle Mann (vcl).   *NYC, October 15, 1928*
BVE 47742-1   BUY, BUY FOR BABY – VOC BM   RCA B&W FXM 1 7283
BVE 47742-3   BUY, BUY FOR BABY – VOC BM   Sunbeam SB 136

IPANA TROUBADOURS
Jimmy McPartland (cnt), Tommy Dorsey (tb), Benny Goodman (cl), unk. tp, as,
ts, p, bjo, tu, d, vcl, S.C. Lanin (dir).   *NYC, October 25, 1928*
W147143-2   DO YOU? THAT'S ALL I WANT TO KNOW – VOC UNK   Sunbeam SB 112

ANNETTE HANSHAW
Mannie Klein (t), Benny Goodman (cl, as), Joe Venuti (v), unk. p, cello, d.
                                            NYC, November 22, 1928
147482-3   I WANNA BE LOVED BY YOU – VOC AH   Sunbeam SB 112
147483-3   IS THERE ANYTHING WRONG IN THAT? – VOC AH   "

THE WHOOPEE MAKERS
as October 15, 1928 except Schumann, Mann out, Ray Bauduc (d) repl. Pollack.
                                             NYC, November, 1928
108513-1   WHOOPEE STOMP   Sunbeam SB 141
3514-A   WHOOPEE STOMP   Sunbeam SB 112
108514-2   BABY   "
108515-2   BUGLE CALL RAG   Sunbeam SB 141

74

BEN POLLACK AND HIS PARK CENTRAL ORCHESTRA

as October 15, 1928 except Gene Austin (vcl) repl Mann.　　*NYC, December 3, 1928*
BVE 49221-3　SENTIMENTAL BABY – VOC GA　　　　RCA B&W FXM 1 7283

THE DIXIE DAISIES

as November Whoopee Makers session except Harris out, Dick McPartland (g)
repl. Morgan.　　　　　　　　　　　　　　　　　　　*NYC, December 23, 1928*
3579-B　　　BLUE LITTLE YOU – voc unk.　　　　　Sunbeam SB 112
3581-C　　　HUNGRY FOR LOVE – voc unk　　　　　　　　　　"

Teagarden repl. by unk. tb., Goodman's presence not definite.
　　　　　　　　　　　　　　　　　　　　　　　　NYC, December 26, 1928
3590-A　　　I'M JUST WONDERING WHO　　　　　　Sunbeam SB 112

THE WHOOPEE MAKERS*

Jimmy McPartland (cnt), Jack Teagarden (tb), Benny Goodman (cl, as), Gil
Rodin (as), Larry Binyon (ts), Vic Briedis (p, cel), Dick Morgan (bjo), Harry
Goodman (b), Ray Bauduc (d).　　　　　　　　　*NYC, December 27, 1928*
108565-3　　FUTURISTIC RHYTHM – VOC MILDRED ROSELLE　　Sunbeam SB 114
108566-1　　OUT WHERE THE BLUES BEGAN – VOC MR　　　　"
108567-1　　RAILROAD MAN – VOC DM　　　　　　　　　　"

*These small groups recorded under a bewildering array of exotic names.
Hereafter, for Sunbeam SB 114, the name of The Whoopee Makers will be used.

add Al Harris (t).　　　　　　　　　　　　　　　*NYC, January 8, 1929*
147759-2　　FUTURISTIC RHYTHM – VOC IRVING KAUFFMAN　　Sunbeam SB 114
147760-2　　LET'S SIT AND TALK ABOUT YOU – VOC IK　　　　"
147761-3　　IN A GREAT BIG WAY – VOC IK　　　　　　　　"

NYC, January, 1929
3261-C　　　THERE'S SOMETHING NEW 'BOUT THE OLD
　　　　　　　MOON TONIGHT – voc unk.　　　　　Sunbeam SB 114

Glenn Miller (tb) repl. Teagarden. Harris and Rodin out.　*NYC, January 18, 1929*
8477-3　　　SHIRT TAIL STOMP　　　　　　　　　Sunbeam SB 141
8478-2　　　ICKY BLUES – VOC DM　　　　　　　　　　"
8478-3　　　ICKY BLUES – VOC DM　　　　　　　　　　"

BEN'S BAD BOYS

as June 4, 1928 except Livingston out, Ray Bauduc (d) repl. Pollack. Goodman cl.
only.　　　　　　　　　　　　　　　　　　　　　*NYC, January 22, 1929*
BVE 49673-1　WANG WANG BLUES　　　　　　　　Sunbeam SB 136
BVE 49674-1　YELLOW DOG BLUES　　　　　　　　　　"
BVE 49675-3　YELLOW DOG BLUES　　　　　　　　　　"

THE WHOOPEE MAKERS
as January 8, 1929 except Rodin out.   *NYC, February, 11, 1929*
8541-1   IT'S TIGHT LIKE THAT   Sunbeam SB 114
8541-2   IT'S TIGHT LIKE THAT   "
8541-3   IT'S TIGHT LIKE THAT   "
8542-1   FOUR OR FIVE TIMES   "
8542-2   FOUR OR FIVE TIMES   "
8542-3   FOUR OR FIVE TIMES   "

BEN POLLACK AND HIS PARK CENTRAL ORCHESTRA
as October 15, 1928 except Ruby Weinstein (t) repl. Harris, Ray Bauduc (d)
repl. Pollack.   *NYC, March 1, 1929*
BVE 50905-2   LOUISE — VOC SMITH BALLEW   RCA B&W FXM 1 7283

NYC, March 5, 1929
BVE 50912-2   MY KINDA LOVE — VOC BEN POLLACK   "
BVE 50913-2   ON WITH THE DANCE! — VOC BP   "

THE WHOOPEE MAKERS
as February 11, 1929 except Harris out, Rodin back in.   *NYC, March 15, 1929*
8477-5   SHIRT TAIL STOMP   Sunbeam SB 114
8542-3   FOUR OR FIVE TIMES — VOC DM   "

NYC, April, 1929
3766-C   DIRTY DOG — VOC JT   Sunbeam SB 141

RED NICHOLS AND HIS FIVE PENNIES
Red Nichols, Leo McConville (t), Jack Teagarden, Glenn Miller (tb), Benny
Goodman (cl), Babe Russin (ts), Jack Russin (p), Carl Kress (g), Artie Miller (b),
Gene Krupa (d).   *NYC, April 18, 1929*
3N133   INDIANA   Affinity AFS 1018
3N134   DINAH   "

BEN POLLACK AND HIS PARK CENTRAL ORCHESTRA
as March 5, 1929.   *NYC, July 25, 1929*
BVE 53949-2   BASHFUL BABY — VOC SCRAPPY LAMBERT   RCA B&W FXM 1 7283,
                                                                         Sunbeam SB 136
BVE 53949-3   BASHFUL BABY — VOC SL   RCA B&W FXM 1 7283

BENNY GOODMAN'S BOYS
Wingy Manone (t), Benny Goodman (cl), Bud Freeman (ts), Joe Sullivan (p),
Herman Foster (bjo), Harry Goodman (tu), Bob Conselman (d).
                                                                         Chicago, August 13, 1929
C 4035   AFTER A WHILE — VOC WM   Sunbeam SB 141, Vocalion VLP2,
                                                                         Affinity AFS 1018
C 4036   MUSKRAT RAMBLE   "

IRVING MILLS AND HIS HOTSY TOTSY GANG

Mannie Klein, Bill Moore (t), Tommy Dorsey (tb), Benny Goodman (cl, as), Jack Pettis (ts, c-mel), Matty Malneck (v), Al Goering (p), Dick McDonough (bjo), Harry Goodman (b), Gene Krupa (d).   *NYC, March 21, 1930*

E 32402	CRAZY 'BOUT MY GAL	Vocalion VLP 2, Decca RAL 508, Affinity AFS 1018
E 32403	RAILROAD MAN	"

HOAGY CARMICHAEL AND HIS ORCHESTRA

Bix Beiderbecke (cnt), Bubber Miley (t), Tommy Dorsey (tb), Benny Goodman (cl), Jimmy Dorsey, Arnold Brilhart (as), Bud Freeman (ts), Joe Venuti (v), Irving Brodsky (p), Hoagy Carmichael (organ–1), Eddie Lang (g), Harry Goodman (b), Gene Krupa (d), Carson Robinson (vcl).   *NYC, May 21, 1930*

BVE 59800-2	ROCKIN' CHAIR(–1) – VOC HC, IB	RCA International INTS 5181
BVE 63301-1	BARNACLE BILL, THE SAILOR – VOC CR, HC, JV	"

RED NICHOLS AND HIS FIVE PENNIES

Red Nichols, Ruby Weinstein, Charlie Teagarden (t), Jack Teagarden, Glenn Miller (tb), Benny Goodman (cl), Sid Stoneburn (as), Babe Russin (as), Jess Stacy (p), Ted Brown (g), Artie Miller (b), Gene Krupa (d).   *NYC, July 3, 1930*

3N181	THE SHEIK OF ARABY	Affinity AFS 1018
3N182	SHIM-ME-SHA-WABBLE	"

RED NICHOLS AND HIS FIVE PENNIES

Red Nichols, Charlie Teagarden (t), Glenn Miller (tb), Benny Goodman (cl), Bud Freeman (ts), Adrian Rollini (bss, xyl), Joe Sullivan (p), Gene Krupa (d).

NYC, August 27, 1930

E 34109-A	CAROLINA IN THE MORNING	Vocalion VLP 2, Decca RAL 508
E 34112	BY THE SHALIMAR	Vocalion VLP 2

BENNY GOODMAN AND HIS ORCHESTRA

Tommy Dorsey or Glenn Miller (tb), Benny Goodman, Sid Stoneburn (cl, as), Larry Binyon (ts), Eddie Lang (g), unk. 2 t, 2 v, p, b, d.   *NYC, November 7, 1930*

E 35341	HE'S NOT WORTH YOUR TEARS – voc unk.	Sunbeam SB 106
E 35344	OVERNIGHT – voc unk.	"

RED AND HIS BIG TEN

Red Nichols, Ruby Weinstein (t), Glenn Miller, Tommy Dorsey (tb), Benny Goodman (cl), Sid Stoneburn (as), Pete Pumiglio (ts), unk. (p), Carl Kress (g), Gene Krupa (d).   *NYC, November 18, 1930*

BVE 64624-3   I'M TICKLED PINK WITH A BLUE-EYED BABY
               – VOC DICK ROBERTSON   RCA B&W RXM 1 7283

RED NICHOLS AND HIS FIVE PENNIES

Red Nichols, Wingy Manone, Charlie Teagarden (t), Glenn Miller (tb), Benny Goodman (cl, bars), Babe Russin (ts), Jack Russin (p), Art Miller (b), Gene Krupa (d).   *NYC, December 10, 1930*

E 35733-A	BUG-A-BOO— voc WM	Vocalion VLP 2
E 35735-A	HOW COME YOU DO ME LIKE YOU DO	
	— voc HAROLD ARLEN	Vocalion VLP 2, Decca RAL 508, Affinity AFS 1018

RED AND HIS BIG TEN

as November 18, 1930.   *NYC, January 5, 1931*

| BVE 67760-1 | AT LAST I'M HAPPY — voc PAUL SMALL | RCA B&W FXM 1 7283 |

GRACE JOHNSTON

Possibly: Ruby Weinstein (t), Tommy Dorsey (tb), Benny Goodman (cl, as), Larry Binyon (ts), Sam Shapiro (v), Arthur Schutt (p).   *NYC, January 13 or 14, 1931*

| E 35920 | EV'RYTHING BUT LOVE — voc GJ | Sunbeam SB 106 |

BEN POLLACK AND HIS ORCHESTRA

Charlie Teagarden, Ruby Weinstein, Sterling Bose (t), Jack Teagarden (tb), Benny Goodman (cl, as), Gil Rodin (as), Eddie Miller (ts), Ed Bergman, Ed Solinsky (v), Bill Schumann (cello), Gil Bowers (p), Nappy Lamare (g), Harry Goodman (b), Ray Bauduc (d).   *NYC, January 21, 1931*

| 10378-2 | SING-SONG GIRL — voc BP | Sunbeam SB 136 |

BENNY GOODMAN AND HIS ORCHESTRA

Possibly: Ruby Weinstein, Charlie Teagarden (t), Glenn Miller (tb), Benny Goodman, Sid Stoneburn (cl, as), Larry Binyon (ts), Sam Shapiro (v), Arthur Schutt(p), Eddie Lang or Dick McDonough (g), Harry Goodman (b), Gene Krupa (d), Paul Small (vcl).   *NYC, February 5, 1931*

| E 35835 | WHEN YOUR LOVER HAS GONE — voc PS | Sunbeam SB 138 |
| E 35838 | MINE YESTERDAY, HIS TODAY — voc PS | Sunbeam SB 106 |

THE CHARLESTON CHASERS

Ruby Weinstein, Charlie Teagarden (t), Jack Teagarden, Glenn Miller (tb), Benny Goodman (cl, as), Sid Stoneburn (as), Larry Binyon (ts), Arthur Schutt (p), Dick McDonough (g), Harry Goodman (b), Gene Krupa (d).

NYC, February 9, 1931

W 151291-2	WALKIN' MY BABY BACK HOME — voc PAUL SMALL	Sunbeam SB 138
W 151292-2	BASIN STREET BLUES — voc JT	Decca RAL 508, Sunbeam SB 138
W 151293-3	BEALE STREET BLUES — voc JT	Sunbeam SB 138

BEN POLLACK AND HIS ORCHESTRA

as January 21, 1931 except Charlie Spivak (t) repl. Charlie Teagarden. Bergman, Solinsky out. add unk. (v).   *NYC, February 12, 1931*

| 10418-1 | I'M A DING DONG DADDY — voc BP | Sunbeam SB 136 |

10416-5	I'VE GOT FIVE DOLLARS — VOC BP	"
10416-6	I'VE GOT FIVE DOLLARS — VOC BP	"
10417-4	SWEET AND HOT — VOC BP, JT, NL	"
10417-5	SWEET AND HOT — VOC BP, JT, NL	"
10422-4	BEALE STREET BLUES — VOC JT	"

BENNY GOODMAN AND HIS ORCHESTRA

Charlie Teagarden (t), Glenn Miller (tb), Benny Goodman (cl, as), Eddie Lang (g), Ray Bauduc (d), plus unk. tp, as, ts, p, b. *NYC, March 18, 1931*

E 36481	WHAT HAVE WE GOT TO DO TONIGHT BUT DANCE — VOC PAUL SMALL	Sunbeam SB 106
E 36482	LITTLE JOE — VOC DICK ROBERTSON	"
E 36483	IT LOOKS LIKE LOVE — VOC PS	"
E 36484	I WANNA BE AROUND MY BABY — VOC PS	"

Bunny Berigan, Mannie Klein (t), Tommy Dorsey (tb), Benny Goodman (cl, as), Sid Stoneburn (as), Larry Binyon (ts, fl), Eddie Lang (g), Gene Krupa (d), unk. p, b, vcl. *NYC, June 20, 1931*

E 36835	SLOW BUT SURE — VOC unk.	Sunbeam SB 106
E 36874	PARDON ME, PRETTY BABY — VOC unk.	"
E 36875	WHAT AM I GONNA DO FOR LOVIN'? — VOC unk.	"
E 36876	YOU CAN'T STOP ME FROM LOVIN' YOU — VOC unk.	"

Charlie Teagarden (t), Glenn Miller (tb), Benny Goodman (cl, as), Sid Stoneburn (as), Larry Binyon (ts), Irving Brodsky (p), Johnny Williams (d), unk. t, g, b, Smith Ballew (vcl). *NYC, September 18, 1931*

W 151794-2	NOT THAT I CARE — VOC SB	Sunbeam SB 138
W 151795-2	HELP YOURSELF TO HAPPINESS — VOC SB	"
W 151796-2	LOVE LETTERS IN THE SAND — SB	"
W 151797-2	I DON'T KNOW WHY — VOC SB	"

Charlie Teagarden, Mannie Klein (t), Jack Teagarden (tb), Benny Goodman (cl), Art Karle (ts), Joe Sullivan (p), Dick McDonough (g), Art Bernstein (b), Gene Krupa (d). *NYC, October 18, 1933*

W 265164-2	I GOTTA RIGHT TO SING THE BLUES — VOC JT	Decca RAL 508, Sunbeam SB 138
W 265165-2	AIN'T-CHA GLAD? — VOC JT	Sunbeam SB 138

Frank Froeba (p) repl. Sullivan. *NYC, October 27, 1933*

W 265166-2	DR HECKLE AND MR JIBE — VOC JT & DM	Sunbeam SB 138
W 265167-2	TEXAS TEA PARTY — VOC JT	"

as October 18, 1933 except Shirley Clay (t) repl. Klein, add Billie Holiday (vcl). *NYC, November 27, 1933*

W 152568-3	YOUR MOTHER'S SON-IN-LAW — VOC BH	Decca RAL 508, Sunbeam SB 138

Holiday out		*NYC, December 4, 1933*
W 152574-2	TAPPIN' THE BARREL — VOC JT	Sunbeam SB 138

as November 27, 1933.		*NYC, December 18, 1933.*
W 152599-2	KEEP ON DOIN' WHAT YOU'RE DOIN' — VOC JT	Sunbeam SB 138
W 152650-2	RIFFIN' THE SCOTCH — VOC BH	"
W 152651-1	LOVE ME OR LEAVE ME	Sunbeam SB 139
W 152652-2	WHY COULDN'T IT BE POOR LITTLE ME?	"

as October 18, 1933 except Charlie Margulis (t), repl. Charlie Teagarden, Sonny Lee (tb) Coleman Hawkins (ts), Arthur Schutt (p) repl. Jack Teagarden, Karle, Sullivan.

		NYC, February 2, 1934
W 152701-3	GEORGIA JUBILEE	Decca RAL 508, Saville SVL 172
		Sunbeam SB 139
W 152702-3	JUNK MAN — VOC MILDRED BAILEY	Decca RAL 508, Saville SVL 172
		Sunbeam SB 139
W 152703-2	OL' PAPPY — VOC MB	Decca RAL 508, Saville SVL 172,
		Sunbeam SB 139
W 152704-2	EMALINE — VOC MB	Sunbeam SB 139, Saville SVL 172

BILL DODGE AND HIS ORCHESTRA

Bunny Berigan, Shirley Clay (t), Joe Harris (tb), Benny Goodman (cl), Hank Ross (ts), Arthur Schutt (p), Dick McDonough (g), Art Bernstein (b), Gene Krupa (d), Red McKenzie (vcl). *NYC, February/March, 1934*

BB 6451	JUNK MAN — VOC RMCK	Hot'n Sweet HOL 6427
	DINAH — VOC RMCK	"
	I GOTTA RIGHT TO SING THE BLUES — VOC RMCK	"
	LOVE IS THE SWEETEST THING — VOC RMCK	"
CBB 6452	I JUST COULDN'T TAKE IT BABY	"
	OL' PAPPY	"
	OLD MAN HARLEM	"
	KEEP ON DOIN' WHAT YOU'RE DOIN'	"
BB 6453	NOBODY'S SWEETHEART NOW	"
	AIN'T-CHA GLAD?	"
	DR HECKLE AND MR JIBE	"
	GEORGIA JUBILEE	"

Mannie Klein (t), Jack Jenney (tb), Art Rollini (ts) repl. Clay, Harris, Ross. *NYC, March, 1934*

BB 6459	TEXAS TEA PARTY	Hot'n Sweet HOL 6427
	HONEYSUCKLE ROSE	"
	HOLIDAY	"
	EMALINE	"

BENNY GOODMAN AND HIS ORCHESTRA

Charlie Teagarden, George Thow (t), Jack Teagarden (tb), Benny Goodman (cl), Hank Ross (ts), Teddy Wilson (p), Benny Martel (g), Harry Goodman (b), Ray McKinley (d).   *NYC, May 14, 1934*

W 152736-1	I AIN'T LAZY-I'M JUST DREAMIN' – VOC JT	Sunbeam SB 139, Saville SVL 172
W 152737-1	AS LONG AS I LIVE – VOC JT	"
W 152738-1	MOONGLOW	Sunbeam SB 139, Decca RAL 508, Saville SVL 172
W 152739-2	BREAKFAST BALL	Sunbeam SB 139, Saville SVL 172

BENNY GOODMAN AND HIS MUSIC HALL ORCHESTRA

Russ Case, Jerry Neary, Sam Shapiro (t), Red Ballard, Jack Lacey (tb), Benny Goodman (cl), Hymie Schertzer, Ben Kantor (as), Art Rollini (ts), Claude Thornhill (p), George Van Eps (g), Hank Wayland (b), Sammy Weiss (d).
NYC, August 16, 1934

CO 15641-1	TAKE MY WORD	Sunbeam SB 139, Saville SVL 172
CO 15642-1	IT HAPPENS TO THE BEST OF FRIENDS – VOC ANN GRAHAM	" "
CO 15643-1	NITWIT SERENADE	Sunbeam SB 139, Saville SVL 172 Decca RAL 508
CO 15644-1	BUGLE CALL RAG	Sunbeam SB 139, Saville SVL 172, Decca RAL 508
CO 15644-2	BUGLE CALL RAG	Sunbeam SB 139

ADRIAN ROLLINI AND HIS ORCHESTRA

poss: Mannie Klein, Dave Klein (t), Jack Teagarden (tb), Benny Goodman (cl), Arthur Rollini (ts, bss), Fulton McGrath (p), George Van Eps (g), Artie Bernstein (b), Stan King (d).   *NYC, October 23, 1934*

6R40	SUGAR	Affinity AFS 1018

BENNY GOODMAN AND HIS MUSIC HALL ORCHESTRA

as before: Harry Goodman (b), Tony Sacco (g) repl. Wayland, Van Eps.
NYC, November 11, 1934

15881-1	LEARNING – VOC TS	Saville SVL 172
15882-1	STARS FELL ON ALABAMA – VOC TS	"
15883-1	SOLITUDE	"
15844-1	I'M GETTING SENTIMENTAL OVER YOU – VOC TS	"

Pee Wee Erwin, Art Sylvester (?) (t), Toots Mondello (as), Frank Froeba (p), George Van Eps (g) repl. Case, Shapiro, Kantor, Thornhill, Sacco. Dick Clark (ts) added.   *NYC, November 26, 1934*

CO 16364-1	I'M A HUNDRED PERCENT FOR YOU – VOC HELEN WARD	Saville SVL 172
CO 16365-1	COKEY	"
CO 16366-1	LIKE A BOLT FROM THE BLUE – VOC BUDDY CLARK	"
CO 16367-1	MUSIC HALL RAG	"

81

BENNY GOODMAN AND HIS ORCHESTRA

Bunny Berigan, Jerry Neary, Art Sylvester (?) (t), Red Ballard, Jack Lacey (tb),
Benny Goodman (cl), Toots Mondello, Hymie Schertzer (as), Art Rollini, Dick
Clark (?) (ts), Frank Froeba (p), George Van Eps (g), Harry Goodman (b), Stan
King (d). *NYC, December 1, 1934 'Let's Dance' b'cast*

THE OBJECT OF MY AFFECTION — VOC BUDDY CLARK	Sunbeam SB 100
WITH EVERY BREATH I TAKE — VOC HELEN WARD	Sunbeam SB 150

NYC, December 8, 1934 'Let's Dance' b'cast

NOT BAD — VOC BC, HW	Sunbeam SB 104
CRAZY RHYTHM — VOC HW	Sunbeam SB 100

as above except Gene Krupa (d) repl. King.

NYC, December 22, 1934 'Lets Dance' b'cast

INDIANA	Sunbeam SB 150
SOLITUDE — VOC HW	,,

as above with Clark certain.

NYC, January 5, 1935 'Let's Dance' b'cast

LET'S DANCE	Sunbeam SB 150
LOVE IS JUST AROUND THE CORNER — VOC BC	Sunbeam SB 100
I'VE GOT A FEELING I'M FALLING VOC HW	Sunbeam SB 105
THE DIXIELAND BAND — VOC HW	Sunbeam SB 104
SERENADE TO A WEALTHY WIDOW	Sunbeam SB 100
STORMY WEATHER — VOC HW	,,
GOOD-BYE	Sunbeam SB 104
THROWIN' STONES AT THE SUN — VOC HW	Sunbeam SB 105
HONEYSUCKLE ROSE	Sunbeam SB 100
LIMEHOUSE BLUES	,,
NIGHT AND DAY — VOC HW	Sunbeam SB 104
BETWEEN THE DEVIL AND THE DEEP BLUE SEA — VOC HW	,,
STARDUST	Sunbeam SB 100

NYC, January 12, 1935 'Let's Dance' b'cast

I'VE GOT A NEW DEAL IN LOVE	Sunbeam SB 150
YOU'RE NOT THE ONLY OYSTER IN THE STEW VOC — HW	
	Sunbeam SB 104

NYC, January 26, 1935 'Lets's Dance' b'cast

I GUESS I'LL HAVE TO CHANGE MY PLANS — VOC HW	Sunbeam SB 100
SWEET AND LOVELY — VOC BARRY MCKINLEY	Sunbeam SB 150
THAT'S A PLENTY	Sunbeam SB 100
AM I BLUE? — VOC HW	Sunbeam SB 104
BASIN STREET BLUES — VOC BMCK	Sunbeam SB 150
BLUE SKIES	Sunbeam SB 104, 150

NYC, February 2, 1935 'Let's Dance' b'cast

I GUESS I'LL HAVE TO CHANGE MY PLANS—VOC HW	Sunbeam SB 150
ST. LOUIS BLUES—VOC HW	Sunbeam SB 105
LOVE ME OR LEAVE ME	Sunbeam SB 104
WHEN WE'RE ALONE—VOC HW	Sunbeam SB 105
MARGIE	Sunbeam SB 104
THE OBJECT OF MY AFFECTION VOC—BMCK	Sunbeam SB 150
BETWEEN THE DEVIL AND THE DEEP BLUE SEA	"
SWEET AND LOVELY—VOC BMCK	Sunbeam SB 105
I'VE GOT THE WORLD ON A STRING—VOC HW	"
CHICAGO	Sunbeam SB 100
SOMEONE TO WATCH OVER ME—VOC HW	Sunbeam SB 150
I CAN'T GIVE YOU ANYTHING BUT LOVE, BABY	Sunbeam SB 100

NYC, February 9, 1935 'Let's Dance' b'cast

I SURRENDER DEAR	Sunbeam SB 104
A NEEDLE IN A HAYSTACK—VOC HW	"
I'M GROWING FONDER OF YOU—VOC BMCK	Sunbeam SB 105
CAN'T WE BE FRIENDS	Sunbeam SB 104

NYC, February 23, 1935 'Let's Dance' b'cast

MAKIN' WHOOPEE	Sunbeam SB 105
THE DARKTOWN STRUTTERS' BALL	Sunbeam SB 150
I WAS LUCKY—VOC HW	"
INDIANA	Sunbeam SB 100

NYC, March 2, 1935 'Let's Dance' b'cast

IF THE MOON TURNS GREEN—VOC BMCK	Sunbeam SB 150
WHAT'S THE REASON—VOC HW	Sunbeam SB 104

NYC, March 9, 1935 'Let's Dance' b'cast

SOLITUDE—VOC HW	Sunbeam SB 100
GOOD-BYE	Sunbeam SB 150

unk. b'cast (poss. April 13, 1935 as follows)

LET'S DANCE	Sunbeam SB 100

NYC, March 27, 1935 'Radio City Matinee' b'cast

ANYTHING GOES—VOC HW	"

NYC, April 13, 1935 'Let's Dance' b'cast

GET HAPPY	Sunbeam SB 104
˙ IT'S AN OLD SOUTHERN CUSTOM—VOC HW	"

83

THE RHYTHM MAKERS

Pee Wee Erwin, Nate Kazebier, Jerry Neary (t), Red Ballard, Jack Lacey (tb), Benny Goodman (cl), Toots Mondello, Hymie Schertzer (as), Art Rollini, Dick Clark (ts), Frank Froeba (p), Allan Reuss (g), Harry Goodman (b), Gene Krupa (d). *NYC, c. June 6, 1935*

MS 92210-1	MAKIN' WHOOPEE	Sunbeam SB 101
	POOR BUTTERFLY	,,
	BALLADE IN BLUE	,,
	BEAUTIFUL CHANGES	,,
MS 92211-1	I WOULD DO MOST ANYTHING FOR YOU	,,
	SOPHISTICATED LADY/MOOD INDIGO	,,
	I CAN'T GIVE YOU ANYTHING BUT LOVE	,,
	YES, WE HAVE NO BANANAS	,,
MS 92212-1	ROSE ROOM	,,
	I NEVER KNEW	,,
	LOVE DROPPED IN FOR TEA	,,
	FAREWELL BLUES	,,
MS 92213-1	PARDON MY LOVE	,,
	I WAS LUCKY	,,
	IF I COULD BE WITH YOU	,,
	DARK TOWN STRUTTERS' BALL	,,
MS 92214-1	ST. LOUIS BLUES	Sunbeam SB 102
	INDIANA	,,
	I SURRENDER DEAR	,,
	BUGLE CALL RAG	,,
MS 92215-1	CAN'T WE BE FRIENDS	,,
	LIFE IS A SONG	,,
	SWEET LITTLE YOU	,,
	BETWEEN THE DEVIL AND THE DEEP BLUE SEA	,,
MS 92216-1	ROYAL GARDEN BLUES	,,
	SWEET AND LOVELY	,,
	THREE LITTLE WORDS	,,
	SUGAR FOOT STOMP	,,
MS 92217-1	WHEN WE'RE ALONE	,,
	THERE MUST HAVE BEEN A DEVIL IN THE MOON	,,
	JINGLE BELLS	,,
	RESTLESS	,,
MS 92218-1	SOMETIMES I'M HAPPY	Sunbeam SB 103
	WRAPPIN' IT UP	,,
	ROSETTA	,,
	YOU CAN DEPEND ON ME	,,
MS 92219-1	ANYTHING GOES	,,
	I GET A KICK OUT OF YOU	,,
	KING PORTER STOMP	,,
	DIGGA DIGGA DOO	,,
MS 92220-1	DOWN BY THE RIVER	,,
	EVERY LITTLE MOMENT	,,

84

	STARDUST	"
	DEAR OLD SOUTHLAND	"
MS 92221-1	I'M A DING DONG DADDY FROM DUMAS	"
	LOVELY TO LOOK AT	"
	SHE'S A LATIN FROM MANHATTAN	"
	I KNOW THAT YOU KNOW	"
MS 92222-1	STOMPIN' AT THE SAVOY	"
	DOWN SOUTH CAMP MEETING	"

BENNY GOODMAN AND HIS ORCHESTRA

as above except Bunny Berigan (t), George Van Eps (g) repl. Erwin, Reuss.
NYC, June 25, 1935

| 92522-1 | BLUE SKIES | RCA B&W PM 45354/NL 89755 |
| 92523 | DEAR OLD SOUTHLAND | " |

Ralph Muzillo (t) repl. Neary.   *NYC, July 1, 1935*

92546-1	SOMETIMES I'M HAPPY	RCA B&W PM 45354/NL 89755,
		RCA Victor VPM 6040
92547-1	KING PORTER STOMP	"
92548-1	BETWEEN THE DEVIL AND THE DEEP	
	BLUE SEA – VOC HW	RCA B&W PM 45354/NL 89755

BENNY GOODMAN TRIO

Benny Goodman (cl), Teddy Wilson (p), Gene Krupa (d).   *NYC, July 13, 1935*

92704-1	AFTER YOU'VE GONE	RCA B&W PM 43176/NL 89753
92704-2	AFTER YOU'VE GONE	"
92705-1	BODY AND SOUL	"
92705-2	BODY AND SOUL	"
92706-1	WHO?	"
92707-1	SOMEDAY, SWEETHEART	"

BENNY GOODMAN AND HIS ORCHESTRA

as July 1, 1935 except Bill De Pew (as), Jess Stacy (p), Allan Reuss (g) repl.
Mondello, Froeba, Van Eps.   *LA (Palomar) August/September, 1935 b'cast*

	STARDUST	Sunbeam SB 105
	BASIN STREET BLUES – VOC JOE HARRIS	"
	GOOD-BYE	"

as above except Joe Harris (tb) repl. Lacey.   *LA, September 27, 1935*

| 97017-2 | MADHOUSE | RCA B&W PM 45354/NL 89755 |

as above except Harry Geller (t) repl. Berigan   *Chicago, November 22, 1935*

96504-1	IF I COULD BE WITH YOU	RCA B&W PM 45354/NL 89755
96505-1	WHEN BUDDHA SMILES	RCA B&W PM 45354/NL 89755,
		RCA Victor VPM 6040

Chicago, December 23, 1935 Congress Hotel b'cast

| | LET'S DANCE | Sunbeam SB 128 |
| | JINGLE BELLS | " |

85

WHERE AM I? — VOC HW		"
REMEMBER		"
THE MUSIC GOES 'ROUND AND 'ROUND VOC JOE HARRIS		"
GET HAPPY		"
BASIN STREET BLUES — VOC JH		"
I'VE GOT A FEELIN' YOU'RE FOOLIN' — VOC HW		"
THAT'S YOUR SWEETHEART — VOC HW		"
LIMEHOUSE BLUES		"
SOMEDAY SWEETHEART		"
GOOD-BYE		"

Chicago, January 6, 1936. Congress Hotel b'cast

LET'S DANCE	Sunbeam SB 129
BLUE SKIES	Sunbeam SB 129, Jazz Live BLJ 8026
WITH ALL MY HEART — VOC HW	"
WALK, JENNY, WALK	"
ROSETTA	"
BUGLE CALL RAG	"
THANKS A MILLION	"
TRUCKIN' — VOC HW	"
ON THE ALAMO	"
EENY MEENY MINEY MO — VOC HW	"
MADHOUSE	"
GOOD-BYE	Sunbeam SB 129

Chicago, January 10, 1936. Congress Hotel b'cast

LET'S DANCE	Sunbeam SB 132
IT'S GREAT TO BE IN LOVE AGAIN — VOC HW	"
REMEMBER	"
I'M GONNA SIT RIGHT DOWN AND WRITE	
MYSELF A LETTER — VOC HW	"
TROUBLESOME TRUMPET — VOC HW	"
ALONE — VOC HW	"
OH, SWEET SUSANNAH — VOC HW	"
GOODY-GOODY — VOC HW	"
TRANSCONTINENTAL	"

Chicago, January 13, 1936. Congress Hotel b'cast

I FEEL LIKE A FEATHER IN THE BREEZE	Sunbeam SB 130
I'M SHOOTING HIGH — VOC HW	"
BIG JOHN SPECIAL	"
DEAR OLD SOUTHLAND	"

Chicago, January 20, 1936. Congress Hotel b'cast

LET'S DANCE	Sunbeam SB 131
FAREWELL BLUES	"

	I'M SHOOTING HIGH — VOC HW	,,
	STOMPIN' AT THE SAVOY	,,
	BASIN STREET BLUES — VOC JH	,,
	I'M BUILDING UP TO AN AWFUL LETDOWN — VOC HW	,,
	TRANSCONTINENTAL	,,
	YOU HIT THE SPOT — VOC HW	,,
	I SURRENDER DEAR	,,
	YANKEE DOODLE NEVER WENT TO TOWN	,,
	HONEYSUCKLE ROSE	,,

Chicago, January 24, 1936.

96568-1	STOMPIN' AT THE SAVOY	RCA B&W PM 45354/NL 89755, RCA Victor VPM 6040
96570-1	BREAKIN' IN A PAIR OF SHOES	RCA B&W PM 45354/NL 89755

Chicago, February 3, 1936. Congress Hotel b'cast

LET'S DANCE	Sunbeam SB 132
DODGING A DIVORCE	,,
THE DAY I LET YOU GET AWAY — VOC HW	,,
SANDMAN	,,
LIGHTS OUT — VOC HW	,,
ALONE — VOC HW	,,
STARDUST	,,
EENY MEENY MINEY MO — VOC HW	,,
KING PORTER STOMP	,,
GOOD-BYE	,,

Chicago, poss. February 19, 1936. Congress Hotel b'cast

DEAR OLD SOUTHLAND	Sunbeam SB 130
LOST	,,
GOODY, GOODY	,,
STARDUST	,,
SANDMAN	,,
I CAN'T GIVE YOU ANYTHING BUT LOVE — VOC HW	,,
ROSETTA	,,
YOU HIT THE SPOT — VOC HW	,,
DIGGA DIGGA DO	,,

GENE KRUPA'S SWING BAND

Roy Eldridge (t), Benny Goodman (cl), Chu Berry (ts), Jess Stacy (p), Allen Reuss (g), Israel Crosby (b), Gene Krupa (d), Helen Ward (vcl).

Chicago, February 29, 1936

BS 100012-1	I HOPE GABRIEL LIKES MY MUSIC	RCA B&W PM 4534/NL 89755
BS 100013-1	MUTINY IN THE PARLOUR — VOC HW	,,
BS 100014-1	I'M GONNA CLAP MY HANDS — VOC HW	,,
BS 100015-1	SWING IS HERE	,,

BENNY GOODMAN AND HIS ORCHESTRA

as prev. full band personnel: *Chicago, March 18, 1936. Congress Hotel b'cast*

	SING, SING, SING – VOC HW	Sunbeam SB 105

BENNY GOODMAN AND HIS ORCHESTRA

Harry Geller, Ralph Muzillo, Nate Kazebier (tp), Red Ballard, Joe Harris (tb), Benny Goodman (cl), Bill de Pew, Hymie Schertzer (as), Art Rollini, Dick Clark (ts), Jess Stacy (p), Allen Reuss (g), Harry Goodman (b), Gene Krupa (d), Helen Ward (vcl)

Chicago, March 20, 1936

100057-1	GET HAPPY	RCA B&W PM 45354/NL 89755
100058-1	CHRISTOPHER COLUMBUS	"
100059-1	I KNOW THAT YOU KNOW	"

RCA Victor VPM 6040

Pee Wee Erwin repl. Muzillo. *Chicago, April 21, 1936 'The Elgin Revue'*

	I'VE FOUND A NEW BABY	Sunbeam SB 105
	PRAIRIE MOON	"

Chicago, April 23, 1936

100379-2	STAR DUST	RCA B&W PM 45354/NL 89755
RE0383-1	REMEMBER	"

BENNY GOODMAN TRIO

Benny Goodman (cl), Teddy Wilson (p), Gene Krupa (d).   *Chicago, April 24, 1936*

100395-1	CHINA BOY	RCA B&W PM 43176/NL 89753
100396-1	MORE THAN YOU KNOW	"
100397-1	ALL M LIFE – VOC HW	"

Chicago, April 27, 1936

100500-1	OH! LADY BE GOOD	RCA B&W PM 43176/NL 89753
100501-1	NOBODY'S SWEETHEART	"
100502-1	TOO GOOD TO BE TRUE – VOC HW	"

BENNY GOODMAN AND HIS ORCHESTRA

as last full band personnel except Gordon 'Chris' Griffin (t), Murray McEachern (tb) repl. Harry Geller, Joe Harris.   *NYC, May 27, 1936*

101255-1	HOUSE HOP	RCA B&W PM 45354/NL 89755
101258-1	I WOULD DO ANYTHING FOR YOU	"

NYC, June 15, 1936

101256-4	THESE FOOLISH THINGS REMIND ME OF YOU – VOC HW	RCA Victor VPM 6040
102215-1	I'VE FOUND A NEW BABY	RCA B&W PM 45354/NL 89755
102217-1	SWINGTIME IN THE ROCKIES	"

as above except Mannie Klein (t) repl. Kazebier, Stacy out (–1).

LA, August 13, 1936

97710-1	YOU TURNED THE TABLES ON ME – VOC HW	RCA Victor VPM 6040
97712-1	PICK YOURSELF UP (–1)	RCA B&W PM 45354/NL 89755
97713-1	DOWN SOUTH CAMP MEETING	RCA B&W PM 45354/NL 89755, RCA Victor VPM 6040

as above except Sterling Bose (t) repl. Klein, add Vido Musso (ts). TRIO titles: Goodman, Wilson, Krupa; QUARTET titles: as Trio plus Lionel Hampton (vib).

LA, August 21, 1936

97748-1	ST. LOUIS BLUES	RCA B&W PM 45354/NL 89755
97750-1	LOVE ME OR LEAVE ME	,,
97751-2	BUGLE CALL RAG	,,
97752-1	MOONGLOW (QUARTET)	RCA B&W PM 43176/NL 89753, RCA Victor VPM 6040

LA, August 26, 1936

97772-1	DINAH (QUARTET)	RCA B&W PM 43176/NL 89753
97773-1	EXACTLY LIKE YOU (TRIO) – VOC LH	,,
97774-1	VIBRAPHONE BLUES (QUARTET) – VOC LH	,,

Zeke Zarchy, Ziggy Elman (t) repl. Bose, Erwin; Clark out, Goodman plays as (–1).

NYC, October 7, 1936

02101-1	ORGAN GRINDER'S SWING	RCA B&W PM 45354/NL 89755
02103-1	RIFFIN' AT THE RITZ (–1)	,,

as above but add Ella Fitzgerald (vcl).

NYC, November 5, 1936

02458-1	SOMEBODY LOVES ME	RCA B&W PM 45354/NL 89755
02459-1	'TAIN'T NO USE – VOC BG	RCA B&W PM 45727/NL 89756
02460-1	BUGLE CALL RAG	RCA B&W PM 45354, NL 89755
02461-1	JAM SESSION	RCA B&W PM 45727/NL 89756
02463-1	GOODNIGHT, MY LOVE – VOC EF	RCA B&W PM 45727/NL 89756, RCA Victor VPM 6040
02464-1	TAKE ANOTHER GUESS – VOC EF	RCA B&W PM 45354, NL 89755
02465-1	DID YOU MEAN IT? – VOC EF	RCA B&W PM 45727/NL 89756

BENNY GOODMAN QUARTET
as before:

NYC, November 18, 1936

03062-1	SWEET SUE, JUST YOU	RCA B&W PM 43176/NL 89753
03063-1	MY MELANCHOLY BABY	,,

BENNY GOODMAN AND HIS ORCHESTRA
NYC, November 25, 1936 b'cast
personnel similar to last

LET'S DANCE	Jazz Archives JA 49
JAM SESSION	,,
'TAIN'T GOOD – VOC HW	,,

89

	MEAN TO ME	„
	GOODNIGHT MY LOVE – VOC HW	„
	SWEET SUE (QUARTET)	„
	PICK YOURSELF UP	„

(Note: other side of Jazz Archives JA 49 by Tommy Dorsey and his Orchestra)

BENNY GOODMAN QUARTET
NYC, December 2, 1936

03064-2	TIGER RAG (TRIO)	RCA B&W PM 43176/NL 89753
03514-1	STOMPIN' AT THE SAVOY	RCA B&W PM 43176/NL 89753,
		Bluebird AXM2-5568
03514-2	STOMPIN' AT THE SAVOY	RCA B&W PM 43176/NL 89753
03515-1	WHISPERING	„

BENNY GOODMAN AND HIS ORCHESTRA
as before except Irving Goodman (t) repl. Zarchy.   *NYC, December 9, 1936*

03549-1	WHEN YOU AND I WERE YOUNG, MAGGIE	RCA B&W PM 45727/
		NL 89756
03552-2	SWING LOW, SWEET CHARIOT	„

as above but add Jimmy Rushing, Margaret McCrae (vcl).   *NYC, December 30, 1936*

03872-1	HE AIN'T GOT RHYTHM – VOC JR	RCA B&W PM 45727/NL 89756
03873-1	NEVER SHOULD HAVE TOLD YOU – VOC MMcC	RCA B&W PM
		44727/NL 89756, RCA Victor VPM 6040

as above except Harry James (t) repl Irving Goodman. Rushing and McCrae out.
NYC, January 14, 1937

04236-1	I WANT TO BE HAPPY	RCA B&W PM 45727/NL 89756
04237-1	CHLO-E	„
04238-1	ROSETTA	„

BENNY GOODMAN QUARTET
as before: *NYC, February 3, 1937*

04559-2	IDA, SWEET AS APPLE CIDER	RCA B&W PM 43176/NL 89753
04560-1	TEA FOR TWO	„
04561-1	RUNNIN' WILD	„

BENNY GOODMAN AND HIS ORCHESTRA
as before except George Koenig (as) repl. De Pew.   *NYC, March 3, 1937*

| | SOMETIMES I'M HAPPY | CBS 54129/30, 66420 |

NYC, March 25, 1937

| | DOWN SOUTH CAMP MEETING | CBS 54129/30, 66420 |

| | RUNNIN' WILD (QUARTET) | „ |

NYC, April 13, 1937
    MINNIE THE MOOCHER'S WEDDING DAY   "

NYC, April 29, 1937
    YOU TURNED THE TABLES ON ME — VOC HW   CBS 54129/30, 66420

NYC, May 11, 1937
    LET'S DANCE   CBS 54129/30, 66420

NYC, June 15, 1937
    THE SHEIK OF ARABY (QUARTET)   CBS 54129/30, 66420

LA, June 29, 1937
    SWEET LEILANI (TRIO)   CBS 54129/30, 66420

LA, July 6, 1937

09569-1	PECKIN'	RCA B&W PM 45727/NL 89756
09570-1	CAN'T WE BE FRIENDS	"
09570-2	CAN'T WE BE FRIENDS	Bluebird AXM2-5568
90571-1	SING, SING, SING PT 1	Bluebird AXM2-5568
90571-2	SING, SING, SING PT 1	RCA B&W PM 45727/NL 89756 RCA Victor VPM 6040
09572-1	SING, SING, SING PT 2	Bluebird AXM2-5568
09572-2	SING, SING, SING PT 2	RCA B&W PM 45727/NL 89756 RCA Victor VPM 6040

same date, LA, 'Camel Caravan' b'cast
    BUGLE CALL RAG   CBS 54129/30, 66420

LA, July 7, 1937

09576-3	ROLL 'EM	RCA B&W PM 45727/NL 89756
09577-1	WHEN IT'S SLEEPY TIME DOWN SOUTH	Bluebird AXM2-5568, RCA B&W PM 45727
09578-1	AFRAID TO DREAM — VOC BETTY VAN	Bluebird AXM2-5568
905778-2	AFRAID TO DREAM — VOC BV	RCA Victor VPM 6040
09579-3	CHANGES	RCA B&W PM 45727/NL 89756

LA, July 13, 1937. 'Camel Caravan' b'cast
    KING PORTER STOMP   CBS 54129/30, 66420

BENNY GOODMAN QUARTET
as before *LA, July 30, 1937*

09627-1	AVALON	RCA B&W PM 43176/NL 89753
09627-2	AVALON	"
09628-1	HANDFUL OF KEYS	"
09628-2	HANDFUL OF KEYS	"
09632-1	THE MAN I LOVE	"

LA, August 2, 1937
09633-2   SMILES   RCA B&W PM 43684/NL 89754
09634-3   LIZA   "

BENNY GOODMAN AND HIS ORCHESTRA
as before: *LA, August 3, 1937 'Camel Caravan' b'cast*
                  ALWAYS   CBS 54129/30, 66420

LA, August 10, 1937. 'Camel Caravan' b'cast
                REMEMBER   Sunbeam SB 146
                ME, MYSELF AND I — VOC BG   "
                SAILBOAT IN THE MOONLIGHT (TRIO)   "
                SHINE (QUARTET)   Sunbeam SB 146, CBS 54129/30, 66420
                SING, SING, SING PT 2   Sunbeam SB 146
Goodman out for next two titles, add Meyer Alexander Chorus
                MOTHER GOOSE MARCHES ON   "
                SWING, BENNY, SWING   "

LA, August 13, 1937 Palomar b'cast
                VIBRAPHONE BLUES (QUARTET) — VOC LH   CBS 54129/30, 66420

LA, August 17, 1937 'Camel Caravan' b'cast
                THAT NAUGHTY WALTZ   Sunbeam SB 146
                SATAN TAKES A HOLIDAY   "
                SO RARE (TRIP)   "
                LIZA   "
                CARAVAN   Sunbeam SB 146, CBS 54129/30, 66420
                GOOD-BYE   CBS 54129/30, 66420
Goodman out for next two titles, add Meyer Alexander Chorus
                LET'S HAVE ANOTHER CIGARETTE   Sunbeam SB 146
                RUSSIAN SWING   "
prob. full band
                CHLO-E   "

LA, August 24, 1937 'Camel Caravan' b'cast
                SOMETIMES I'M HAPPY   Sunbeam SB 147
                MINNIE THE MOOCHER'S WEDDING DAY   "
                MY CABIN OF DREAMS (TRIO)   "
                STOMPIN' AT THE SAVOY (QUARTET)   "
                SAILBOAT IN THE MOONLIGHT — VOC MARTHA TILTON   "
                ROLL 'EM   "
Goodman out for next two titles, add Meyer Alexander Chorus, Pat O'Malley (vcl-1)
                BYE, BYE, PRETTY BABY   "
                SWING HIGH, SWING LOW (-1)   "

LA, August 31, 1937 'Camel Caravan' b'cast

	CAMEL HOP	"
	LA CUCARACHA	"
	WHISPERS IN THE DARK (TRIO)	"
	THE BLUE DANUBE — VOC MA CHORUS	"
	VIBRAPHONE BLUES (QUARTET) — VOC LH	"
	SWING SONG — VOC MA CHORUS, PO'M	"
	THE DIXIELAND BAND — VOC MT	"
	HOUSE HOP	"

LA, September 6, 1937

09633-2	BOB WHITE — VOC MARTHA TILTON	RCA B&W PM 45727/
		NL89756
09689-1	SUGAR FOOT STOMP	RCA B&W PM 45727/
		NL 89756, RCA Victor VPM 6040
09689-2	SUGAR FOOT STOMP	Bluebird AXM2-5568
09690-2	I CAN'T GIVE YOU ANYTHING BUT LOVE BABY — VOC MT	
		RCA B&W PM 45727/NL 89756
09691-1	MINNIE THE MOOCHER'S WEDDING DAY	"

Dallas, September 14, 1937 'Camel Caravan' b'cast

| | PECKIN' | CBS 54129/30, 66420 |

Vernon Brown (tb) repl McEachern.   *NYC, October 2, 1937 b'cast*

| | RIDIN' HIGH | CBS 54129/30, 66420 |

Gene Goodman (tp) repl. Elman *NYC, October 13, 1937 b'cast*

	LET'S DANCE	Sunbeam SB 116
	IN THE SHADE OF THE OLD APPLE TREE	"
	THAT OLD FEELING — VOC MT	"
	MOONLIGHT ON THE HIGHWAY	"
	WHISPERS IN THE DARK (TRIO)	"
	THE MOON GOT IN MY EYES — VOC MT	"
	CHLO-E	"
	AVALON (QUARTET PLUS BAND)	"
	I'D LIKE TO SEE SOME MORE OF SAMOA — VOC MT	"
	CARAVAN	"
	SATAN TAKES A HOLIDAY	"
	GOOD-BYE	"

NYC, October 16, 1937 b'cast

	LET'S DANCE	Sunbeam SB 117
	HOUSE HOP	"
	SO MANY MEMORIES — VOC MT	"
	MY HONEY'S LOVIN' ARMS	"
	BOB WHITE — MT	"
	ROSES IN DECEMBER (TRIO)	"

93

	MARIE	,,
	DING DONG DADDY (QUARTET)	,,
	LOCH LOMOND — VOC MT	,,
	ROLL 'EM	,,

Ziggy Elman (tp) repl. Gene Goodman.

NYC, October 19, 1937 'Camel Caravan' b'cast

| | SUNNY DISPOSISH | CBS 54129/30, 66420 |
| | EVERYBODY LOVES MY BABY | ,, |

NYC, October 20, 1937 b'cast

	STARDUST ON THE MOON — VOC MT	Sunbeam SB 118
	DEAR OLD SOUTHLAND	,,
	SO MANY MEMORIES — VOC MT	,,
	ONE O'CLOCK JUMP	,,
	BODY AND SOUL (TRIO)	,,
	ME, MYSELF AND I — VOC MT	,,
	SWEET SUE (QUARTET)	,,
	WHEN IT'S SLEEPY TIME DOWN SOUTH	,,
	CAMEL HOP	,,

NYC, October 21, 1937 b'cast

	LET'S DANCE	Sunbeam SB 119
	MINNIE THE MOOCHER'S WEDDING DAY	,,
	AFRAID TO DREAM — VOC MT	,,
	MOONLIGHT ON THE HIGHWAY	,,
	ONCE IN A WHILE — VOC MT	,,
	SUGAR FOOT STOMP	,,
	MORE THAN YOU KNOW	,,
	THE DIXIELAND BAND — VOC MT	,,

Murray McEachern (tb) repl. Brown. *NYC, October 22, 1937*

| 015535-1 | LET THAT BE A LESSON TO YOU — VOCMT | RCA B&W PM 45727/ NL89756 |
| 015538-1 | POP-CORN MAN — VOC MT | ,, |

Brown repl. McEachern *NYC, October 23, 1937 b'cast*

	LET'S DANCE	Sunbeam SB 120
	IN THE SHADE OF THE OLD APPLE TREE	,,
	YOU'RE MY DESIRE — VOC MT	,,
	AM I BLUE?	,,
	WHERE OR WHEN (TRIO)	,,
	SOMEDAY SWEETHEART	,,
	BOB WHITE — VOC MT	,,
	NAGASAKI (QUARTET)	,,
	YOURS AND MINE — VOC MT	,,

NYC, October 27, 1937 b'cast

LET'S DANCE	Sunbeam SB 121
WHEN BUDDHA SMILES	"
CHERRY	"
SWING LOW, SWEET CHARIOT	"
STAR DUST	"
THE LADY IS A TRAMP — VOC MT	"
A HANDFUL OF KEYS (QUARTET)	"
SO MANY MEMORIES — VOC MT	"
SWINGTIME IN THE ROCKIES	"

NYC, October 29, 1937

015575-1	WHERE OR WHEN (TRIO)	RCA B&W PM 43684/NL 89754
015576-1	SILHOUETTED IN THE MOONLIGHT (TRIO) — VOC MT	"
015577-2	VIENI, VIENI (QUARTET)	"

NYC, October 30, 1937 b'cast

LET'S DANCE	Sunbeam SB 122
MAKING WHOOPEE	"
FAREWELL MY LOVE — VOC MT	"
THE LADY IS A TRAMP — VOC MT	"
OH! LADY BE GOOD (TRIO)	"
LOVE ME OR LEAVE ME	"
ONCE IN A WHILE — VOC MT	"
EVERYBODY LOVES MY BABY (QUARTET)	"
YOU AND I KNOW — VOC MT	"

NYC, November 2, 1937 'Camel Caravan' b'cast

TIME ON MY HANDS (TRIO)	CBS 54129/30, 66420

NYC, November 3, 1937 b'cast

AT THE DARKTOWN STRUTTERS' BALL	CBS 54129/30, 66420

NYC, November 4, 1937 b'cast

LET'S DANCE	Sunbeam SB 123
CHANGES	"
IF IT'S THE LAST THING I DO — MT	"
SOMEDAY SWEETHEART	"
SO MANY MEMORIES	"
LIFE GOES TO A PARTY	"
FAREWELL MY LOVE — VOC MT	"
IN THE SHADE OF THE OLD APPLE TREE	"
BLOSSOMS ON BROADWAY — VOC MT	"
WALK, JENNY, WALK	"
I CAN'T GIVE YOU ANYTHING BUT LOVE, BABY — VOCMT	"

NYC, November, 6, 1937 b'cast

LET'S DANCE	Sunbeam SB 127
THAT NAUGHTY WALTZ	"
ONCE IN A WHILE — VOC MT	"
MORE THAN YOU KNOW (TRIO)	"
POP-CORN MAN — VOC MT	"
YOU SHOWED ME THE WAY — VOC MT	Sunbeam SB 124
BLUE SKIES	"
VIENI, VIENI (QUARTET)	"
IF IT'S THE LAST THING I DO — VOC MT	"
LIFE GOES TO A PARTY	"
GOOD-BYE	"

Will Bradley (tb) repl. Brown.   *NYC, November 9, 1937 'Camel Caravan' b'cast*
         SOMEDAY SWEEETHEART   CBS 54129/30, 66420

Murray McEachern repl. Bradley.   *NYC, November 12, 1937*

017041-1	LOCH LOMOND — VOC BG, MT	RCA B&W PM 45727/NL 89756
017042-1	CAMEL HOP	"
017043-2	TRUE CONFESSION — VOC MT	"
017044-2	LIFE GOES TO A PARTY	"

Bradley repl. McEachern.   *NYC, November 16, 1937 'Camel Caravan' b'cast*
         NAGASAKI (QUARTET)   CBS 54129/30, 66420

Brown repl. Bradley.   *NYC, November 19, 1937 b'cast*
         STAR DUST   CBS 54129/30, 66420

NYC, November 20, 1937 b'cast

LET'S DANCE	Sunbeam SB 125
LAUGHING AT LIFE	"
YOU TOOK THE WORDS RIGHT OUT OF MY HEART — VOC MT	"
SWEET STRANGER — VOC MT	"
WHO? (TRIO)	"
DOWN SOUTH CAMP MEETING	"
IN THE STILL OF THE NIGHT — VOC MT	"
LIMEHOUSE BLUES (QUARTET)	"
MAMA, THAT MOON IS HERE AGAIN — VOC MT	"
SWINGTIME IN THE ROCKIES	"
FARWELL MY LOVE — VOC MT	"

NYC, November 21, 1937 b'cast
         ST. LOUIS BLUES   CBS 54129/30, 66420

Will Bradley (tb) repl. Brown.   *NYC, November 23, 1937 'Camel Caravan' b'cast*
         CLARINET MARMALADE   CBS 54129/30, 66420

NICE WORK IF YOU CAN GET IT (TRIO)　　CBS 54129/30, 66420, 21064

NYC, November 30, 1937 'Camel Caravan' b'cast
    ST. LOUIS BLUES　　　　　　　　　　　　　　　　　　"
    MOONGLOW (QUARTET)　　　　　　　　　　　　　"

Vernon Brown (tb) repl. Bradley.　　　　　　　　*NYC, December 2, 1937*
017044-3　　LIFE GOES TO A PARTY　　　　RCA B&W PM 45727/NL 89756
017045-1　　I'M A DING DONG DADDY (QUARTET)　　RCA B&W PM 43684/
　　　　　　　　　　　　　　　　　NL 89754, Bluebird AXM2-5568

017045-2　　I'M A DING DONG DADDY (QUARTET)　　　　　　　"
017452-1　　IT'S WONDERFUL — VOC MT　　RCA B&W PM 45272/NL 89756
017453-1　　THANKS FOR THE MEMORY — VOC MT　　　　　　"

NYC, December 3, 1937
017454-1　　IF DREAMS COME TRUE　　　　RCA B&W PM 45727/NL 89756
017456-1　　SWEET STRANGER — VOC MT　　　　　　　　　"

NYC, December 7, 1937 'Camel Caravan' b'cast
    HAVE YOU MET MISS JONES? (TRIO)　　　　CBS 54129/30, 66420
    KILLER DILLER (QUARTET)　　　　　　　CBS 54129/30, 66420

Babe Russin (ts) repl. Musso.　　*NYC, December 14, 1937 'Camel Caravan' b'cast*
    JOSEPHINE　　　　　　　　　　　　CBS 54129/30, 66420
    MY GAL SAL (QUARTET)　　　　　　　CBS 54129/30, 66420

NYC, December 16, 1937 b'cast
    ONE O'CLOCK JUMP　　　　　　　　　　Sunbeam SB 127

NYC, December 18, 1937 b'cast
    LET'S DANCE　　　　　　　　　　　　Sunbeam SB 126
    BIG JOHN SPECIAL　　　　　　　　　　　　　"
    YOU TOOK THE WORDS RIGHT OUT OF MY HEART — VOC MT　　"
    IF DREAMS COME TRUE　　　　　　　　　　　　"
    BEI MIR BIST DU SCHOEN — VOC MT　　　　　　　"
    WHERE OR WHEN (TRIO)　　　　　　　　　　　"
    AT THE DARKTOWN STRUTTERS BALL　　　　　　"
    I HITCHED MY WAGON TO A STAR — VOCMT　　　　"
    DINAH (QUARTET)　　　　　　　　　　　　"
    I WANNA BE IN WINCHELL'S COLUMN — VOC MT　　"
    ALL OF ME　　　　　　　　　　　　　　　"

NYC, December 21, 1937
017754-1　　BEI MIR BIST DU SCHOEN PT 1
　　　　　　(QUARTET) — VOC MT　　　　RCA B&W PM 43684/NL 89754
017754-2　　BEI MIR BIST DU SCHOEN PT 1
　　　　　　(QUARTET) — VOC MT　　　　　　　　　　　"

NYC, December 22, 1937 b'cast

LIFE GOES TO A PARTY	Sunbeam SB 127
SWEET SOMEONE – VOC MT	"
IF DREAMS COME TRUE	Sunbeam SB 124
CAN'T HELP LOVIN' THAT MAN (TRIO)	"
GOOD-BYE	"
SWEET ALICE BLUE GOWN	"
JOSEPHINE	"
IT'S WONDERFUL – VOC MT	"
AVALON (QUARTET PLUS BAND)	"
ROCKIN' THE TOWN – VOC MT	"

NYC, December 29, 1937

017783-1	BEI MIR BIST DU SCHOEN PT 2 (QUARTET PLUS ZIGGY ELMAN) –	
	VOC MT	RCA B&W PM 43684/NL 89754

BENNY GOODMAN AND HIS ORCHESTRA

Harry James, Ziggy Elman, Chris Griffin (t), Red Ballard, Vernon Brown (tb), Benny Goodman (cl), Hymie Schertzer, George Koenig (as), Art Rollini, Babe Russin (ts), Jess Stacy (p), Allen Reuss (g), Harry Goodman (b), Gene Krupa (d). TRIO: Goodman, Teddy Wilson (p), Krupa.
QUARTET: Goodman, Wilson, Krupa, Lionel Hampton (vib).

NYC January 16, 1938 Carnegie Hall

DON'T BE THAT WAY	CBS 66202, 66420
SOMETIMES I'M HAPPY	Sunbeam SB 127
ONE O'CLOCK JUMP	CBS 66202, 66420

Griffin, Brown, Goodman, Stacy, Krupa only:

SENSATION RAG	"

Bobby Hackett (t), Brown, Goodman, Russin, Stacy, Reuss, Krupa only:

I'M COMING VIRGINIA	"

Griffin, Brown, Goodman, Stacy, Krupa only:

WHEN MY BABY SMILES AT ME	"

Full band:

SHINE	"

Cootie Williams (t), Goodman, Johnny Hodges (as), Harry Carney (bars), Stacy, Reuss, Krupa:

BLUE REVERIE	"

Full band:

LIFE GOES TO A PARTY	"

James, Buck Clayton (t), Brown, Goodman, Hodges, Lester Young (ts), Carney, Count Basie (p), Freddie Green (g), Walter Page (b), Krupa:

HONEYSUCKLE ROSE	"

Full band, Trio, Quartet:

BODY AND SOUL (TRIO)	"
AVALON (QUARTET)	"

98

THE MAN I LOVE (QUARTET)		CBS 66202, 66420
I GOT RHYTHM (QUARTET)		CBS 66202, 66420, 21064
BLUE SKIES		CBS 66202, 66420
LOCH LOMOND – VOC MT		,,
BLUE ROOM		,,
SWINGTIME IN THE ROCKIES		,,
BEI MIR BIST DU SCHOEN – VOC MT		,,
CHINA BOY (TRIO)		,,
STOMPIN' AT THE SAVOY (TRIO)		,,
DIZZY SPELLS (QUARTET)		,,
SING, SING, SING		,,
IF DREAMS COME TRUE		Sunbeam SB 127
BIG JOHN SPECIAL		CBS 66202, 66420

NYC, January 29, 1938 b'cast
I'M A DING DONG DADDY (QUARTET)		CBS 54129/30, 66420

NYC, February 15, 1938 'Camel Caravan' b'cast
ROLL 'EM		CBS 54129/30, 66420

NYC, February 16, 1938
019831-1	DON'T BE THAT WAY	RCA Victor VPM 6040, RCA NL 89587
019832-1	ONE O'CLOCK JUMP	,,

Dave Matthews (as), Lester Young (ts), Freddie Green (g), Walter Page (b), Lionel Hampton (d) repl. Koenig, Rollini, Reuss, Harry Goodman, Krupa.
NYC, March 9, 1938
021127-1	PLEASE BE KIND – VOC MT	RCA NL 89587
021128-1	TI-PI-TIN	,,
021129-1	OOOOOH-OH-BOOM! – VOC MT, BG	,,
021130-1	ALWAYS AND ALWAYS – VOC MT	,,
021131-1	MAKE BELIEVE	,,
021132-2	BLUE ROOM	RCA NL 89587, Bluebird AXM2-5568

Trio and Quartet: Dave Tough (d) repl. Krupa
021625-1	SWEET LORRAINE (TRIO)	RCA B&W PM 43684/NL 89754
021626-1	THE BLUES IN YOUR FLAT (QUARTET)	,,
021626-2	THE BLUES IN YOUR FLAT (QUARTET)	,,
021627-1	THE BLUES IN MY FLAT (QUARTET) – VOC LH	RCA B&W PM 43684/ NL 89754
021628-1	SUGAR (QUARTET)	RCA B&W PM 43684/NL 89754 Bluebird AXM2-5568
021628-2	SUGAR (QUARTET)	RCA B&W PM 43684/NL 89754
021629-1	DIZZY SPELLS (QUARTET)	,,

Full band as February 16, 1938 except Dave Matthews, Milt Yaner (as), Bud Freeman (ts), Ben Heller (g), Dave Tough (d) repl. Schertzer, Koenig, Russin, Reuss, Krupa. *NYC, April 8, 1938*

022415-1	LULLABY IN RHYTHM	Bluebird AXM2-5566
022415-2	LULLABY IN RHYTHM	Bluebird AXM2-5568, RCA NL 89587
022416-1	I NEVER KNEW	Bluebird AXM2-5566, RCA NL 89587
022417-1	THAT FEELING IS GONE — VOC MT	Bluebird AXM2-5566
022419-1	SWEET SUE, JUST YOU	Bluebird AXM2-5566, RCA NL 89587

Noni Bernardi (as) repl. Yaner. *NYC, April 22, 1938*

022487-1	I LET A SONG GO OUT OF MY HEART — VOC MT	Bluebird AXM2-5566, RCA Victor VPM 6040
022488-1	WHY'D YA MAKE ME FALL IN LOVE? — VOC MT	Bluebird AXM2-5566, RCA NL 89587
022418-3	FEELIN' HIGH AND HAPPY — VOC MT	"

NYC , May 28, 1938

023506-1	DON'T WAKE UP MY HEART — VOC MT	Bluebird AXM2-5566
023507-1	I'VE BEEN SAVING MYSELF FOR YOU — VOC MT	"
023508-1	BIG JOHN SPECIAL	Bluebird AXM2-5566, RCA NL 89587
023509-1	MY MELANCHOLY BABY	Bluebird AXM2-5566
023509-2	MY MELANCHOLY BABY	Bluebird AXM2-5568
023510-1	WRAPPIN' IT UP	Bluebird AXM2-5566
023510-2	WRAPPIN' IT UP	Bluebird AXM2-5568, RCA NL 89587
023511-1	WHAT GOES ON HERE IN MY HEART? — VOC MT	Bluebird AXM2-5566

NYC, May 31, 1938

| 023517-2 | A LITTLE KISS IN THE TWILIGHT — VOC MT | Bluebird AXM2-5566 |
| 023518-2 | THE FLAT FOOT FLOOGIE — VOC BAND | Bluebird AXM2-5566, RCA NL 89587 |

Boston, Mass, June 14, 1938 'Camel Caravan' b'cast

| | I HADN'T ANYONE TILL YOU — VOC MT | CBS 54129/30, 66420 |

NYC, July 11, 1938

| 024020-2 | I'VE GOT A DATE WITH A DREAM — VOC MT | Bluebird AXM2-5566 |
| 024021-2 | COULD YOU PASS IN LOVE? — VOC MT | " |

Full band: Lionel Hampton (d) repl. Tough. *NYC, August 8, 1938*

| 024473-2 | BLUE INTERLUDE — VOC MT | Bluebird AXM2-5566 |

Tough repl. Hampton, Rollini out. *NYC, August 12, 1938*

| 024498-1 | WHEN I GO A-DREAMIN' — VOC MT | " |

Detroit, August 30, 1938 'Camel Caravan' b'cast

| | BENNY SENT ME | CBS 54129/30, 66420 |

100

Chicago, September 12, 1938
025466-1	YOU'RE A SWEET LITTLE HEADACHE — VOC MT	**Bluebird AXM2-5566**
025467-1	I HAVE EYES — VOC MT	"

Chicago, September 14, 1938
025476-1	MARGIE	**Bluebird AXM2-5566, RCA NL 89587**
025477-1	WHAT HAVE YOU GOT THAT GETS ME? — VOC MT	**Bluebird AXM2-5566**
025478-1	RUSSIAN LULLABY	**Bluebird AXM2-5566, RCA NL 89587**

Chicago, October 12, 1938
025876-1	OPUS ½ (QUARTET)	**Bluebird AXM2-5566, RCA B&W PM 43684**
025877-1	I MUST HAVE THAT MAN (TRIO)	"
025878-2	SWEET GEORGIA BROWN (QUARTET)	"
025879-1	'S WONDERFUL (QUARTET)	"
025879-2	'S WONDERFUL (QUARTET)	**Bluebird AXM2-5568, RCA B&W PM 43684**

Chicago, October 13, 1938
025468-3	YOU'RE LOVELY, MADAME — VOC MT	**Bluebird AXM2-5566**
025475-3	I HAD TO DO IT — VOC MT	"
025798-1	IS THAT THE WAY TO TREAT A SWEETHEART? — VOC MT	"
025799-1	BUMBLE BEE STOMP	**Bluebird AXM2-5566, RCA NL 89587**
025900-1	CIRIBIRIBIN	**Bluebird AXM2-5567**
025901-1	THIS CAN'T BE LOVE — VOC MT	"

Full band: Hampton (d) repl. Tough.   *NYC, November 10, 1938*
028942-1	SING FOR YOUR SUPPER — VOC MT	**Bluebird AXM2-5567**
028943-1	TOPSY	**Bluebird AXM2-5567, RCA NL 89587**
028944-1	SMOKE HOUSE	**Bluebird AXM2-5567**
028944-2	SMOKE HOUSE	**Bluebird AXM2-5568, RCA NL 89587**

Buddy Schutz (d) repl. Hampton.   *NYC, November 23, 1938*
028997-2	I MUST SEE ANNIE TONIGHT — VOC MT	**Bluebird AXM2-5567**
028998-2	KINDA LONESOME — VOC MT	"
028999-1	MY HONEY'S LOVIN' ARMS	"
028999-2	MY HONEY'S LOVIN' ARMS	**Bluebird AXM2-5568, RCA NL 89587**
030308-1	FAREWELL BLUES	**Bluebird AXM2-5567**
030308-2	FAREWELL BLUES	**Bluebird AXM2-5568, RCA NL 89587**

Jerry Jerome (ts) repl. Freeman.   *NYC, December 12, 1938*
030390-1	IT HAD TO BE YOU	**Bluebird AXM2-5567**
030390-2	IT HAD TO BE YOU	**Bluebird AXM2-5568, RCA NL 89587**
030391-1	LOUISE	**Bluebird AXM2-5567**
030391-2	LOUISE	**Bluebird AXM2-5568**

NYC, December 15, 1938

030701-1	WHISPERING	Bluebird AXM2-5567, RCA NL 89587
030702-2	BACH GOES TO TOWN	"
030703-1	I'LL ALWAYS BE IN LOVE WITH YOU	"
030704-1	UNDECIDED	"

NYC, December 23, 1938

030760-1	WE'LL NEVER KNOW—VOC MT	Bluebird AXM2-5567
030761-1	GOOD FOR NOTHIN' BUT LOVE—VOC MT	"

BENNY GOODMAN QUINTET
Goodman, Hampton, Wilson, John Kirby (b), Schutz   *NYC, December 29, 1938*

030774-1	PICK-A-RIB PT 1	Bluebird AXM2-5567, RCA B&W PM 43684
030774-2	PICK-A-RIB PT 1	RCA B&W PM 43684
030775-1	PICK-A-RIB PT 2	Bluebird AXM2-5567, RCA B&W PM 43684
030775-2	PICK-A-RIB PT 2	RCA B&W PM 43684
030776-1	I CRIED FOR YOU	Bluebird AXM2-5568, RCA B&W PM 43684
030776-2	I CRIED FOR YOU	Bluebird AXM2-5567, RCA B&W PM 43684

BENNY GOODMAN QUARTET
Goodman, Wilson, Kirby, Hampton (d), Same session.

030777-1	I KNOW THAT YOU KNOW	Bluebird AXM2-5568, RCA B&W PM 43684
030777-2	I KNOW THAT YOU KNOW	Bluebird AXM2-5567, RCA B&W PM 43684

BENNY GOODMAN AND HIS ORCHESTRA
Full band. Add Meade Lux Lewis (p–1), Albert Ammons (p–2), Johnny Mercer
(v)   *NYC, January 3, 1939 'Camel Caravan' b'cast*

LET'S DANCE	Giants of Jazz GOJ 1030
I CAN'T GIVE YOU ANYTHING BUT LOVE, BABY	"
HURRY HOME—VOC MT	"
THE SONG WRITER'S STORY—VOC JM	"
YOU MUST HAVE BEEN A BEAUTIFUL BABY—VOC JM,BG	"
HONKY TONK TRAIN BLUES (–1)	"
CUCKOO IN THE CLOCK—VOC JM	"
ROLL 'EM (–1,–2)	"
GOOD-BYE	"

Lewis, Ammons out. Leonard Ware (g), al Hall (b) on Sextet titles only.
                          NYC, January 10, 1939 'Camel Caravan' b'cast

LET'S DANCE	Giants of Jazz GOJ 1030
SWEET SUE	"
COULD BE—VOC MT, JM, BG	"
SOFTLY AS IN A MORNING SUNRISE (TRIO:	
GOODMAN, WILSON, HAMPTON (d)	"

	CIRIBIRIBIN	"
	I HAVE EYES – VOC MT	"
	UMBRELLA MAN (SEXTET: GOODMAN, WILSON, HAMPTON (vib),	
	LEONARD WARE (g), AL HALL (b), SCHUTZ)	"
	SENT FOR YESTERDAY – VOC JM	"
	GOOD-BYE	"

METRONOME ALL STAR BAND

Charlie Spivak, Bunny Berigan, Sonny Dunham (t), Tommy Dorsey, Jack Teagarden (tb), Benny Goodman (cl), Hymie Schertzer (as), Eddie Miller, Art Rollini (ts), Bob Zurke (p), Carmen Mastren (g), Bob Haggart (b), Ray Bauduc (d).   *NYC, January 11, 1939*

BS 031445-2	BLUE LOU	Bluebird AXM2-5568
BS 031445-3	BLUE LOU	"

Harry James (t) repl. Spivak. *NYC, January 12, 1939*
BS 031446-1	THE BLUES	Bluebird AXM2-5568

BENNY GOODMAN AND HIS ORCHESTRA

As January 10 without guest instrumentalists. Irving Goodman (t), Hymie Schertzer (as) repl. James, Matthews.   *NYC, February 1, 1939*

031873-1	GOTTA GET SHUT-EYE – VOC MT	Bluebird AXM2-5567
031874-1	CUCKOO IN THE CLOCK – VOC JOHNNY MERCER	"
031875-1	AND THE ANGELS SING – VOC MT	Bluebird AXM2-5567, RCA Victor VPM 6040, RCA NL 89587
031876-1	SENT FOR YOU YESTERDAY – VOC JM	Bluebird AXM2-5567, RCA NL 89587

Hartford, February 7, 1939 'Camel Caravan' b'cast
	LET'S DANCE	Giants of Jazz GOJ 1033
	SWINGING DOWN THE LAND	"
	GOTTA GET SOME SHUT EYE – VOC MT	"
	I FOUND A NEW BABY (QUARTET)	"
	ESTRELLITA	"
	CUCKOO IN THE CLOCK – VOC MT	"
	EVERYBODY KNOWS THOSE OLD JOKES – VOC JM, BG	"
	HARTFORD STOMP	"
	GOOD-BYE	"

NYC, February 9, 1939
033710-1	ESTRELLITA	Bluebird AXM2-5567
033711-1	A HOME IN THE CLOUDS – VOC MT	"

Philadelphia, February 14, 1939 'Camel Caravan' b'cast
	LET'S DANCE	Giants of Jazz GOJ 1033
	UNDECIDED	"
	A HOME IN THE CLOUDS – VOC MT	"

TREES	"
SWEEET LITTLE HEADACHE — VOC MT	"
DEEP PURPLE (QUARTET)	"
HOLD TIGHT	"
COULD BE — VOC MT, JM, BG	"
SENT FOR YOU YESTERDAY	"
GOOD-BYE	"

NYC April 6, 1939
035708-1   OPUS ¾   RCA B&W PM 43684/NL 89754, Bluebird
                                       AXM2-5567

NYC, April 7, 1939
035713-1	SHOW YOUR LINEN, MISS RICHARDSON — VOC JM	Bluebird AXM2-5567
035714-1	THE LADY'S IN LOVE WITH YOU — VOC MT	"
035716-1	THE KINGDOM OF SWING	"
035716-2	THE KINGDOM OF SWING	Bluebird AXM2-5568, RCA NL 89587
035717-1	ROSE OF WASHINGTON SQUARE	Bluebird AXM2-5567
035718-1	THE SIREN'S SONG	Bluebird AXM2-5568

Corky Cornelius (t), Lionel Hampton (d) repl. I. Goodman, Schutz. Bruce Squires (tb) added. Either Quinn Wilson or Art Bernstein (b) repl. H. Goodman.   *Chicago, May 4, 1939*
034649-1	PICK-A-RIB	Bluebird AXM2-5568
		RCA NL 89587
034650-1	YOU AND YOUR LOVE — VOC MT	Bluebird AXM2-5568
034651-2	WHO'LL BUY MY BUBLITCHKI?	"

Until RCA completes its reissue programme the studio sessions can be traced through albums which draw primarily upon alternate takes. These include Phontastic NOST 7605, 7606, 7612, 7615, 7616, 7617, 7620, 7644, 7648, 7650, 7652, 7654, Blu-disc T 1012, Jazz Society AA 510, Black Lion 127 034.

Ziggy Elman, Jimmy Maxwell, Johnny Martel (t), Red Ballard, Vernon Brown, Ted Vesely (tb), Benny Goodman (cl), Toots Mondello, Buff Estes (as), Bus Bassey, Jerry Jerome (ts), Fletcher Henderson (p), Arnold Covey (g), Art Bernstein (b), Nick Fatool (d).   *NYC, September 13, 1939*
CO 25355   I'VE BEEN THRERE BEFORE - VOC LOUISE TOBIN   Phontastic
                                                               NOST 7610

BENNY GOODMAN SEXTET
Benny Goodman (cl), Lionel Hampton (vib, Fletcher Henderson (p), Charlie Christian (g), Art Bernstein (b), Nick Fatool (d).   *NYC, October 2, 1939*
WCO 26132 A	FLYING HOME	CBS BPG 62581
WCO 26132 B	FLYING HOME	Phontastic NOST 7610
WCO 26133	ROSE ROOM	CBS BPG 62581

WCO 26134   STARDUST   "

BENNY GOODMAN AND HIS ORCHESTRA
Lionel Hampton (d) repl. Fatool; Sextet as above; Trio: Goodman, Henderson,
Hampton (d).   *NYC, October 6, 1939 Carnegie Hall*

	DON'T BE THAT WAY	Collector's Classics CC 18
	SUNRISE SERENADE	"
	T'AIN'T WHAT YOU DO	"
	BACH GOES TO TOWN	"
	ONE O'CLOCK JUMP	"
	SHEIK OF ARABY (TRIO)	"
	FLYING HOME (SEXTET)	"
	STARDUST (SEXTET)	"
	SING, SING, SING	"

Nick Fatool (d) repl. Hampton   *NYC, October 20, 1939*
WCO 26194   MAKE WITH THE KISSES —
             VOC MILDRED BAILEY   Phontastic NOST 7610

NYC, prob. October 23, 1939 b'cast
             MEMORIES OF YOU (SEXTET)   Jazz Archives JA 42

NYC, November 22, 1939
WCO 26284   MEMORIES OF YOU (SEXTET)   CBS BPG 62581
WCO 26285 A SOFT WINDS (SEXTET)   CBS 52538
WCO 26285 B SOFT WINDS (SEXTET)   Phontastic NOST 7610
WCO 26286   SEVEN COME ELEVEN (SEXTET)   CBS 52538
WCO 26287   DARN THAT DREAM —
             VOC MB   Phontastic NOST 7610
WCO 26289   BEYOND THE MOON   "
Add Charlie Christian (g)   *same date*
WCO 26290   HONEYSUCKLE ROSE   CBS BPG 62581

BENNY GOODMAN SEXTET
NYC, November 27, 1939 b'cast
             AC-DC CURRENT   MGM 2367 407

NYC, prob. December 2, 1939 'Camel Caravan' b'cast
             AC-DC CURRENT   Jazz Archives JA 42

Johnny Guarnieri (p) repl. Henderson.   *NYC, December 20, 1939*
WCO 26354 A SHIVERS   CBS BPG 62581
WCO 26354 B SHIVERS   Blu-disc T 1012
WCO 26355   AC-DC CURRENT   CBS 52538
WCO 26356   I'M CONFESSIN'   Phontastic NOST 7610

NYC, prob.December 31, 1939 b'cast

TILL TOM SPECIAL   Jazz Archives JA 42

BENNY GOODMAN AND HIS ORCHESTRA
Johnny Guarnieri (p) repl. Henderson.   *NYC, January 16, 1940*
WCO 26419   SQUEEZE ME   Phontastic NOST 7610

METRONOME ALL STAR BAND
Charlie Spivak, Ziggy Elman, Harry James (t), Jack Teagarden, Jack Jenney (tb), Benny Goodman (cl), Toots Mondello, Benny Carter (as), Eddie Miller, Charlie Barnet (ts), Jess Stacy (p), Charlie Christian (g), Bob Haggart (b), Gene Krupa (d).

NYC, February 7, 1940
WCO 26489 B   KING PORTER STOMP   Phontastic NOST 7610,
                                                     Blu-disc T 1012

METRONOME ALL STAR NINE
James, Teagarden, Goodman, Carter, Miller, Stacy, Christian, Haggart, Krupa.   *Same date.*
WCO 26490 B   ALL STAR STRUT   Blu-disc T 1012

BENNY GOODMAN SEXTET
Count Basie (p) repl. Guarnieri.   *Same date as Metronome session*
WCO 26494   TILL TOM SPECIAL   CBS 52538
WCO 26495   GONE WITH WHAT WIND   "

Guarnieri (p) repl. Basie.   *NYC, April 10, 1940*
WCO 26718   SHEIK OF ARABY   CBS BPG 62581
WCO 26719   POOR BUTTERFLY   CBS 52538

BENNY GOODMAN AND HIS ORCHESTRA
Irving Goodman (t), Les Robinson (as), Charlie Christian (g) repl. Martel, Estes, Covey.   *NYC, April 16, 1940*
WCO 26739   I CAN'T LOVE YOU ANYMORE –
             VOC HELEN FORREST   Phontastic NOST 7610
WCO 26743   I SURRENDER, DEAR (SEXTET)   CBS BPG 62581
WCO 26744   BOY MEETS GOY (SEXTET)   "

LA, May 9, 1940
WCO 26807   WHO CARES – VOC FRED ASTAIRE   CBS 21064

Dudley Brooks (p) repl. Guarnieri.   *LA, June 20, 1940*
WCO 26940   SIX APPEAL (SEXTET)   CBS 52538

LA, July 3, 1940
WCO 26983   NOSTALGIA   Phontastic NOST 7610

BENNY GOODMAN SEXTET

(In fact eight musicians are listed, giving rise to doubt of correct personnel.) Buck Clayton (t), Benny Goodman (cl), Lester Young (ts), Count Basie (p), Charlie Christian, Freddie Green (g), Walter Page (b), Jo Jones (d).   *NYC, October 28, 1940*

	BLUES	Jazz Archives JA 6, JA 42
		Jazz Document VA 7997
	I NEVER KNEW	"
	DICKIE'S DREAM (CHARLIE'S DREAM)	"
	WHOLLY CATS	"
	DICKIE'S DREAM (LESTER'S DREAM)	"

BENNY GOODMAN AND HIS SEXTET

Cootie Williams (t), Benny Goodman (cl), Georgie Auld (ts), Count Basie (p), Charlie Christian (g), Art Bernstein (b), Harry Jaeger (d).   *NYC, November 7, 1940*

CO 29027-1	WHOLLY CATS	Jazz Archives JA 6, Jazz
		Document VA 7997, CBS 52538
CO 29027-2	WHOLLY CATS	Jazz Document VA 7997
CO 29028-1	ROYAL GARDEN BLUES	Jazz Archives JA 6, Jazz
		Document VA 7997, CBS BPG 62581
CO 29029-1	AS LONG AS I LIVE	CBS BPG 62581
CO 29030-1	BENNY'S BUGLE Jazz Archives JA6, Jazz Document VA 7997, CBS
		BPG 62581

BENNY GOODMAN AND HIS ORCHESTRA

Alec Fila, Jimmy Maxwell, Irving Goodman (t), Cootie Williams (tp–1), Lou McGarity, Red Gingler (tb), Benny Goodman (cl), Skippy Martin, Gus Bivona, Bob Snyder (as), Georgie Auld, Jack Henderson (ts), Bernie Leighton (p), Fletcher Henderson (p–2), Mike Bryan (g), Art Bernstein (b), Harry Jaeger (d), Helen Forrest (vcl).   *NYC, November 13, 1940*

CO 29062	NOBODY (–1)	Phontastic NOST 7610
CO 29063-1	THE MAN I LOVE – VOC HF	"
CO 29063-2	THE MAN I LOVE – VOC HF	CBS 21064
CO 29064	HENDERSON STOMP (–1, –2)	Phontastic NOST 7610
CO 29065	BENNY RIDES AGAIN (–1)	"

Cutty Cutshall (tb) repl. Gingler.   *NYC, N ·ιember 29, 1940*

| CO 29178 | CABIN IN THE SKY – VOC HF | Phontastic NOST 7610 |

BENNY GOODMAN SEXTET

as November 7, 1940 except Ken Kersey (p) repl. Basie.   *NYC, December 19, 1940*

CO 29259-reh.i	BREAKFAST FEUD	Jazz Archives JA6
CO 29259-reh.ii	BREAKFAST FEUD	"
CO 29259	BREAKFAST FEUD	"
CO 29260-1	I CAN'T GIVE YOU ANYTHING BUT LOVE, BABY	CBS BPG 62581
CO 29260-2	I CAN'T GIVE YOU ANYTHING BUT LOVE, BABY	Jazz Archives JA 6
CO 29260-3	I CAN'T GIVE YOU ANYTHING BUT LOVE, BABY	"
CO 29261-1	GILLY	CBS 52538

CO 29261-2   GILLY   Jazz Archives JA 6

BENNY GOODMAN SEXTET
Basie (p), Jo Jones (d) repl. Kersey, Jaeger.   *NYC, January 15, 1941*
CO 29512-
  spliced   BREAKFAST FEUD   CBS 52538
CO 29513   ON THE ALAMO   CBS BPG 62581
CO 29514   I FOUND A NEW BABY   "
CO 29519-1   GONE WITH WHAT DRAFT   CBS 52538
CO 29519-2   GONE WITH WHAT DRAFT   Jazz Archives JA 6

Snyder out, Pete Mondello repl. Henderson, rhythm section: Johnny Guarnieri
(p), Charlie Christian (g), Art Bernstein (b), Dave Tough (d).
                                                   NYC, March 4, 1941
CO 29865-1   SOLO FLIGHT   CBS BPG 62581
CO 29865-2   SOLO FLIGHT   CBS 52538

BENNY GOODMAN SEXTET
Cootie Williams (t), Benny Goodman (cl, not on first two titles), Georgie Auld (ts),
Johnny Guarnieri (p), Charlie Christian (g), Art Bernstein (b), Dave Tough
(d).   *NYC, March 13, 1941*
            BLUES IN B   CBS 52538
            WAITIN' FOR BENNY   "
CO 29942   A SMO-O-O-OTH ONE   "

BENNY GOODMAN AND HIS ORCHESTRA
Billy Butterfield, Jimmy Maxwell, Cootie Williams (t), Lou McGarity, Cutty
Cutshall (tb), Benny Goodman (cl), Clint Neagley, Gene Kinsey (as), Vido Musso,
Pete Mondello (ts), Skippy Martin (bars), Mel Powell (p), Tom Morgan (g),
Walter Iooss (b), Sid Catlett (d), Helen Forrest (vcl).   *Atlantic City, July 1941 b'cast*
            ROLL 'EM   Honeysuckle Rose HR 5004/5
            DON'T BE THAT WAY   "

add Al Davis (tp), George Berg, Chuck Gentry, John Simmons repl. Mondello,
Martin, Iooss.   *Chicago, July 25, 1941 b'cast*
            FLYING HOME   Honeysuckle Rose HR 5004/5

Skippy Martin, Peggy Lee repl. Kinsey, Forrest.   *Chicago, August 15, 1941*
CCO 3950-2   ELMER'S TUNE – VOC PL   CBS 32417

Chicago, August 20, 1941 b'cast
            THE EARL   Joyce LP 1056
            IT'S SO PEACEFUL IN THE COUNTRY   "
            DELILAH   "
            TIME WAS   "
            TUESDAY AT TEN   "
            INTERMEZZO   "

BENNY RIDES AGAIN   "

Gene Kinsey, Mark Blitz repl. Martin, Simmons. Add Tommy Taylor (vcl).
Meadowbrook, N.J., September 11, 1941 b'cast
    TUESDAY AT TEN   Honeysuckle rose HR 5004/5
    WHEN THE SUN COMES OUT   "
    A SMO-O-O-OTH ONE   "
    ROLL 'EM (COMPOSITE)   "

Meadowbrook, N.J., September 14, 1941 b'cast
    BENNY RIDES AGAIN   Honeysuckle Rose HR 5004/5
    TAKE IT   "
    CONCERTO FOR COOTIE   "

Meadowbrook, N.J., September 16, 1941 b'cast
    THE COUNT   Honeysuckle Rose HR 5004/5
    SMOKE GETS IN YOUR EYES   "
    THE EARL   "
    BIRTH OF THE BLUES   "
    POUND RIDGE   "
    ROLL 'EM   "
Meadowbrook, N.J., September 20, 1941 b'cast
    BENNY RIDES AGAIN   "

Meadowbrook, N.J., September 23, 1941 b'cast
    THE EARL   "
    IF IT'S TRUE   "
    ONE O'CLOCK JUMP   "

Mort Stuhlmaker repl. Blitz, Catlett out.   *NYC, September 25, 1941*
CO 31366-1 THAT'S THE WAY IT GOES –
         VOC PL   CBS 32417

Blitz repl. Stuhlmaker, Catlett returns.   *Meadowbrook, N.J., October 1, 1941, b'cast*
    SING, SING, SING   Honeysuckle Rose HR 5004/5

NYC, October 2, 1941
CO 31392-1 MY OLD FLAME – VOC PL   CBS 32417

Meadowbrook, N.J., October 4, 1941 b'cast
    IDA (TRIO: GOODMAN, POWELL,
        CATLETT)   Honeysuckle Rose HR 5004/5

Meadowbrook, N.J., October 8, 1941 b'cast
    CLARINET A LA KING   "
    I'M HERE   "
    DON'T LET THE DOORKNOB HITCHA   "

Sid Weiss, Ralph Collier, Julie Schwartz repl. Blitz, Catlett, Martin. Williams
out.   *NYC, November 13, 1941*
CO 31743-2   HOW LONG HAS THIS BEEN GOING ON? –
               VOC PL   CBS 21064, 32417
CO 31744-1   THAT DID IT, MARIE –
               VOC PL   CBS 32417

Bernie Privin, Sol Kane repl. Butterfield, Schwartz.   *NYC, December 10, 1941*
CO 31945-1   NOT A CARE IN THE WORLD –
               VOC PL   CBS 32417

METRONOME ALL STAR BAND
Harry James, Cootie Williams, Roy Eldrige (t), J.C.Higginbotham, Lou McGarity
(tb), Benny Goodman (cl), Toots Mondello, Benny Carter (as), Vido Musso, Tex
Beneke (ts), Count Basie (p), Freddie Green (g) Doc Goldberg (b), Gene Krupa
(d).   *NYC, December 31, 1941*
CO 32079   ROYAL FLUSH   Phontastic NOST 7620
CO 32080   DEAR OLD SOUTHLAND   „
CO 32080   DEAR OLD SOUTHLAND   „

BENNY GOODMAN AND HIS ORCHESTRA
Johnny Napton (t), Bud Shiffman (as) repl. Davis, Neagley.   *NYC, March 12, 1942*
CO 32601-1   I THREW A KISS IN THE OCEAN –
               VOC PL   CBS 32417
CO 32602-1   WE'LL MEET AGAIN –
               VOC PL   „
CO 32603-1   FULL MOON – VOC PL   „

Charlie Castaldo (tb), Alvin Stoller (d) repl. Cutshall, Collier.   *NYC, May 14, 1942*
CO 32794-1   ALL I NEED IS YOU – VOC PL   „

possible personnel: Lee Castaldo, Ray Linn, Bobby Guyer, Jimmy Pupa (t), Miff
Mole, Charlie Castaldo (tb), Benny Goodman (cl), Hymie Schertzer, Leonard
Kaye (as), John Walton, Bob Taylor (ts), Joe Rushton (bars), Jess Stacy (p), Bart
Roth (g), Gus Van Camp (b), Louis Bellson (d).   *Unk. location, March, 1943 b'cast*
               WHY DON'T YOU DO RIGHT? – VOC PL   Swing House SWH 46
               I LOVE A PIANO – VOC PL, BG   „

poss. similar. *Unk. location, date, 1943 b'cast*
               AIR MAIL SPECIAL   Swing House SWH 46
               STEALIN' APPLES   „

Ralph Muzillo, Lee Castaldo, Bobby Guyer (t), Bill Harris, Al Mastren (tb),
Benny Goodman (cl), Hymie Schertzer, Eddie Rosa (as), Bob Taylor, Herbie
Haymer (ts), Joe Rushton (bars), Jess Stacy (p), Allen Reuss (g), Sid Weiss (b),
Gene Krupa (d).   *Unk. location, 1943 b'cast*
               AFTER YOU'VE GONE   Swing House SWH 46

110

I'M JUST WILD ABOUT HARRY   "

Springfield, September 29, 1943 b'cast
    SUGARFOOT STOMP   Queen Disc 042, Swing
                                                      Treasury 103

    CLARINET A LA KING   Swing Treasury 103
    I'VE FOUND A NEW BABY   "
    SWEET GEORGIA BROWN (QUINTET:
    GOODMAN PLUS RHYTHM SECTION)   Queen Disc 041, Swing
                                                      Treasury 103

Charlie Frankenhauser (t), Mark Bennett (tb), Al Klink (ts), Ernie Caceres (bars),
repl. Guyer, Mastren, Haymer, Rushton.   *NYC, October 13, 1943 b'cast*
    MISSION TO MOSCOW   Queen Disc 042, Swing
                                                      Treasury 103
    YOU'RE DRIVING ME CRAZY   Swing Treasury 103
    HENDERSON STOMP   Queen Disc 042
    DO NOTHING TILL YOU HEAR FROM ME –
    VOC BG   "
    OH! LADY BE GOOD. (TRIO:
    GOODMAN, STACY, KRUPA)   "
    STEALIN' APPLES   Swing Treasury 103

NYC, October 21, 1943 b'cast
    MINNIE'S IN THE MONEY – VOC BG   Queen Disc 042
    DON'T BE THAT WAY   "
    STEALIN' APPLES   "
    I'M JUST WILD ABOUT HARRY   "

H.Collins (tb), Leonard Kaye (as), Zoot Sims (ts) repl. Bennett, Rosa, Taylor.
                        Prob. NYC, November 5, 1943 b'cast
    MISSION TO MOSCOW   Swing Treasury 103

NYC, November 9, 1943 b'cast
    I'M HERE   Queen Disc 042
    DO NOTHING TILL YOU HERE FROM ME   Swing Treasury 103
    HENDERSON STOMP   "
    SING, SING, SING   "

NYC, November 17, 1943 b'cast
    HONEYSUCKLE ROSE (TRIO)   Queen Disc 042

NYC, November 27, 1943 b'cast
    HONEYSUCKLE ROSE (QUARTET:
    GOODMAN, STACY, WEISS, KRUPA)   Swing Treasury 103

Prob.similar personnel. Unk.locations prob. around NYC. Unknown dates prob. between November-December, 1943

DOWN SOUTH CAMP MEETING	Swing Treasury 103
I'LL BE AROUND— VOC CAROL KAY	"
SEVEN COME ELEVEN	"
KING PORTER STOMP	"
HENDERSON STOMP	Swing House SWH 46, Jazz Society AA 509
THREE LITTLE WORDS (QUARTET)	"
I FOUND A NEW BABY	Swing House SWH 46
LIMEHOUSE BLUES (TRIO)	Jazz Society AA 509

Annapolis, December 16, 1943

SEVEN COME ELEVEN	Queen Disc 042

BENNY GOODMAN QUARTET
Benny Goodman (cl), Jess Stacy (p), Sid Weiss (b), Morey Feld (d),
LA, January 18, 1944 b'cast

RACHEL'S DREAM	Swing House SWH 46

BENNY GOODMAN AND HIS ORCHESTRA
Johnny Dee, Frank Bernardi, Charlie Frankenhauser (?), Mickey Mangano (t), Bill Harris, Al Mastren (tb), Benny Goodman (cl), Heinie Beau, Eddie Rosa (as), Al Klink, Zoot Sims (ts), Eddie Beau (bars), Jess Stacy (p), Allen Reuss (g), Sid Weiss (b), Morey Feld (d), Lorraine Elliott (vcl). *LA, February, 1944*

TEN DAYS WITH BABY— VOC LE	Swing House SWH 46, Jazz Society AA 509
RACHEL'S DREAM (GOODMAN PLUS RHYTHM)	Jazz Society AA 509

BENNY GOODMAN AND HIS ORCHESTRA
Billy Butterfield, Charlie Shavers, Mickey McMickle (t), Vernon Brown, Jack Satterfield (tb), Benny Goodman (cl), Hymie Schertzer, Jules Rubin (as), Art Rollini, Don Byas (ts), Ernie Caceres (bars), Teddy Wilson (p). Allen Reuss (g), Sid Weiss (b), Cozy Cole (d). *NYC, June 12, 1944*

1245	ALL THE CATS JOIN IN	Capitol 5C05280854

BENNY GOODMAN TRIO
Goodman, Wilson, Specs Powell (d). *NYC, June, 1944 b'cast*

POOR BUTTERFLY	Jazz Society AA 509
THE WORLD IS WAITING FOR THE SUNRISE	"

BENNY GOODMAN AND HIS V-DISC ALL STAR BAND
Yank Lawson, Roy Eldridge, Mickey McMickle (t), Vernon Brown, Ward Silloway (tb), Benny Goodman (cl), Hymie Schertzer, Reggie Merrill (as), Art Rollini, Wolfe Tayne (ts), Ernie Caceres (bars), Teddy Wilson (p), Tommy Kay (g), Gene Traxler (b), Specs Powell (d). *NYC, July 31, 1944*

D4-TC-290-1C	THESE FOOLISH THINGS — VOC MILDRED BAILEY	Jazz Society AA 509

112

D4-TC-290-1C HALLELUJAH (QUARTET:
 GOODMAN, WILSON, TRAXLER, POWELL)   Jazz Society AA 509,
    Swing House SWH 46

Prob. same personnel.   *NYC, July/August, 1944 (V-Disc matrix nos. suggest this session took place before July 31).*
D4-TC-283-1 AFTER YOU'VE GONE   Jazz Society AA 509
D4-TC-285-1 THERE'LL BE A JUBILEE –
    VOC MB   "

BENNY GOODMAN QUINTET
Benny Goodman (cl), Red Norvo (vib), Teddy Wilson (p), Sid Weiss (b), Morey
Feld (d).   *NYC, October, 1944*
D4-TC-444-1 SWEET GEORGIA BROWN   Jazz Society AA 509
D4-TC-444-1A SHEIK OF ARABY   "
D4-TC-446-1A BLUES   "
D4-TC-447-1 ROSE ROOM   "

BENNY GOODMAN TRIO
Benny Goodman (cl), Alec Templeton (p), Morey Feld (d).
    NYC, November 6, 1944 b'cast
    IMPROVISATION   Swing House SWH 46

Bernie Privin, John Best, Nate Kazebier, Jimmy Blake or Dick Mains (t), Lou
McGarity, Cutty Cutshall (tb), Addison Collins (Fr-h), Benny Goodman (cl), John
Prager, Bill Shine or Larry Molinelli (as), Gish Gilbertson, Cliff Strickland (ts),
Danny Bank or Ralph LoPollo (bars), Mel Powell (p), Mike Bryan (g), Barney
Spieler (b) Louis Bellson (d), Art Lund (voc).   *NYC, May 28, 1946 b'cast*
    I'VE GOT THE SUN IN THE MORNING –
    VOC AL   Swing House SWH 46

BENNY GOODMAN SEXTET
Benny Goodman (cl), Johnny White (vib), Mel Powell (p), Mike Bryan (g), Jack
Lesberg (b), Louis Bellson (d).   *NYC, July 1, 1946 b'cast*
    I GOT RHYTHM   Swing House SWH 17

BENNY GOODMAN AND HIS ORCHESTRA
Hymie Schertzer (as), John Pepper (bars), Joe Bushkin (p), Jack Lesberg (b) repl.
Prager, Bank, Powell, Spieler.   *NYC, July 18, 1946*
CO 36659   FLY BY NIGHT   Phontastic NOST 7654

poss. Spieler back for Lesberg
NYC, same day b'cast
    SOMETIMES I'M HAPPY – VOC EVE YOUNG   Swing House SWH 17

113

Lesberg back
NYC, July 22, 1946 b'cast

　　　　　　　　TIGER RAG　　　　　　　　　　　　　　Swing House SWH 17
Mike McMickle (t), Leon Cox (tb), Lester Clark (ts), Al Klink (bars), Barney
Spieler (b) repl. Privin, McGarity, Gilbertson, Pepper, Lesberg.

　　　　　　　　　　　　　　　　　　　　　　　　NYC, August 7, 1946
CO 36738　　　PUT THAT KISS BACK WHERE YOU FOUND IT –

　　　　　　　　VOC BG, ART LUND　　　　　　　　Phontastic NOST 7654
CO 36739　　　MY BLUE HEAVEN　　　　　　　　　　　"

NYC, August 12, 1947

　　　　　　　　RACHEL'S DREAM　　　　　　　　　Swing House SWH 17

NYC, September 2, 1946 b'cast

　　　　　　　　SHINE　　　　　　　　　　　　　　Swing House SWH 17

LA, September 23, 1946 b'cast

　　　　　　　　I WANT TO GO WHERE YOU GO　　　　Swing House SWH 3

Barney Kessel (g), Harry Babasin (b) repl. Bryan, Spieler.　　*LA, October 7, 1946*

　　　　　　　　THE SHEIK OF ARABY　　　　　　　Swing House SWH 3

　　　　　　　　ST. LOUIS BLUES　　　　　　　　　Swing House SWH 17

LA, October 14, 1946 b'cast

　　　　　　　　HONEYSUCKLE ROSE　　　　　　　　Swing House SWH 3

LA, October 21, 1946 b'cast

　　　　　　　　I'LL ALWAYS BE IN LOVE WITH YOU　　Swing House SWH 3

NYC, October 28, 1946 b'cast

　　　　　　　　FLYING HOME　　　　　　　　　　Swing House SWH 3

NYC, November 11, 1946 b'cast

　　　　　　　　RED HORSE BOOGIE WOOGIE　　　　Swing House SWH 3

BENNY GOODMAN QUINTET
White out. Jess Stacy (p), Sammy Weiss (d) repl. Bushkin, Bellson.

　　　　　　　　　　　　　　　　　　　LA, January 6, 1947 b'cast

　　　　　　　　SLIPPED DISC　　　　　　　　　　Swing House SWH 17
LA, January 13, 1947

　　　　　　　　I'LL ALWAYS BE IN LOVE WITH YOU　　Swing House SWH 17
Benny Goodman (cl), Ernie Felice (accordian), Jess Stacy (p), Harry Babasin (b),
Tommy Romersa (d).　　　　　　　　　　　　　*LA, February 12, 1947*
1632　　　　I'LL ALWAYS BE IN LOVE WITH YOU　　Capitol VMPM 1002

BENNY GOODMAN SEXTET
as Quintet, add Allen Reuss (g).　　　　　　　　　　*LA, March 10, 1947*

　　　　　　　　YOU TURNED THE TABLES ON ME –

　　　　　　　　VOC BERYL DAVIS　　　　　　　　Swing House SWH 17

BENNY GOODMAN QUINTET
as above, Reuss out.   *same date*
                    FINE AND DANDY   Swing House SWH 17

BENNY GOODMAN SEXTET
Benny Goodman (cl), Ernie Felice (accordian), Jimmy Rowles (p), Al Hendrickson
(g), Harry Babasin (b), Tommy Romersa (d).   *LA, March 31, 1947*
                    THE BANISTER SLIDE   Swing House SWH 17
                    PUTTIN' ON THE RITZ   "

Add Red Norvo (vib), Felice out, Don Lamond (d) repl. Romersa.
                                                          LA, April 7, 1947
                    HOW HIGH THE MOON   Swing House SWH 17

BENNY GOODMAN TRIO
Benny Goodman (cl), Jimmy Rowles (p), Tommy Romersa (d). *LA, April 21, 1947*
                    UP A LAZY RIVER   Swing House SWH 3

BENNY GOODMAN AND HIS ORCHESTRA
John Best, Nate Kazebier, George Seaburg, Frank Beach (t), Lou McGarity, Ray
Simms, Tommy Pederson (tb), Benny Goodman (cl), Gus Bivona, Heinie Beau
(as), Babe Russin, Zoot Sims (ts), Chuck Gentry (bars), Tommy Todd (p), Al
Hendrickson (b), Harry Babasin (b), Tommy Romersa (d).   *LA, April 24, 1947*
1873   TATTLETALE   Capitol VMPM 1002

THE HOLLYWOOD HUCKSTERS
Charlie Shavers (t), Benny Goodman (cl), Benny Carter (as), Dave Cavanaugh
(ts), Joe Kock (bars), Red Norvo (vib, xyl), Jimmy Rowles (p), Irving Ashby (g),
Red Callender (b), Lee Young (d).   *LA, May 29, 1947*
2007   THEM THERE EYES   Capitol VMPM 1002
2008   HAPPY BLUES— VOC BG AND STAN KENTON   '

BENNY GOODMAN AND HIS ORCHESTRA
as April 24, 1947; Irving Goodman (t), Hoyt Bohannon (tb), Herbie Haymer,
Stan Getz (ts) Jimmy Rowles (p), Don Lamond (d) repl. Kazebier, Simms, Russin,
Sims, Todd, Romersa.   *LA, June 5, 1947*
2023   EIGHT, NINE AND TEN PT. 2   Capitol VMPM 1002
2024   THE BEST THINGS IN LIFE ARE FREE —
                    VOC LILIAN LANE   "

BENNY GOODMAN SEXTET
Benny Goodman (cl), Red Norvo (vib), Jimmy Rowles (p), Al Hendrickson (g),
Harry Babasin (b), Don Lamond (d).   *LA, June 23, 1947*
                    SWEET GEORGIA BROWN   Swing House SWH 17

Mel Powell (p), Art Shapiro (b), Louis Bellson (d) repl. Rowles, Babasin, Lamond.   *LA, August 25, 1947*
2198   NAGASAKI   Capitol VMPM 1002

Joe Mondragon (b), Tommy Romersa (d) repl. Shapiro, Bellson.
                                                    LA, September 22, 1947
2261   VARSITY DRAG   Capitol VMPM 1002

BENNY GOODMAN TRIO
Benny Goodman (cl), Teddy Wilson (p), Jimmy Crawford (d).
                                                    NYC, November 7, 1947
1996   BLUE AND BROKEN HEARTED   Capitol VMPM 1002
1999   I'LL NEVER BE THE SAME   ,,

Same: *NYC, November 17, 1947*
2520   STOMPIN' AT THE SAVOY   ,,

BENNY GOODMAN AND HIS ORCHESTRA
John Best, Jake Porter, Irving Goodman, Ray Linn (t), Hoyt Bohannon, Herb Harper, Tommy Pederson (tb), Benny Goodman (cl), Jack Kelson, Nick Mumolo (as), Pete Pumiglio, Bump Meyers (ts), Chuck Gentry (bars), Mel Powell (p), Al Hendrickson (g), Red Callender (b), Bill Douglass (d), Emma Lou Welch (vcl).   *LA, December 23, 1947*
3055   MUSKRAT RAMBLE   Capitol VMPM 1002
3056   AM I BLUE — VOC ELW   ,,

BENNY GOODMAN QUINTET
Benny Goodman (cl), Red Norvo (vib), Mel Powell (p), Red Callender (b), Lee Young (d), Johnny Mercer (vcl).   *LA, January, 1948*
              AIRMAIL SPECIAL   Swing House SWH 3
              THE WORLD IS WAITING FOR THE SUNRISE   ,,
              ROSE ROOM   ,,
              FLYING HOME   ,,
              SENT FOR YOU YESTERDAY —
              VOC JM   ,,

BENNY GOODMAN SEPTET
Benny Goodman, Stan Hasselgaard (cl), Wardell Gray (ts), Teddy Wilson (p), Billy Bauer (g), Arnold Fishkind (b), Mel Zelnick (d).
                                        Philadelphia, June 3, 1948 b'cast
              MEL'S IDEA   Dragon DRLP 29

Mary Lou Williams (p), Clyde Lombardi (b) repl. Wilson, Fishkind.
                                        White Plains, June 26, 1948 b'cast
              SWEDISH PASTRY   Dragon DRLP 29

White Plains, July 3, 1948
MEL'S IDEA   Dragon DRLP 29

Fats Navarro (t), Benny Goodman (cl), Wardell Gray (ts), Gene Di Novi (p),
Mundell Lowe (g), Clyde Lombardi (b), Mel Zelnick (d).   *LA, September 9, 1948*
2974   STEALIN' APPLES   Capitol 5C 052 80 854

BENNY GOODMAN AND HIS ORCHESTRA
Doug Mettome, Howard Reich, Al Stewart, Nick Travis (t), Milt Bernhart, Eddie
Bert, George Monte (tb), Benny Goodman (cl), Angelo Cicalese, Mitch Goldberg
(as), Wardell Gray, Eddie Wasserman (ts), Larry Molinelli (bars), Buddy Greco
(p), Francis Beecher (g), Clyde Lombardi (b), Sonny Igoe (d).
                                                    LA, February 10, 1949
3958   UNDERCURRENT BLUES   Capitol 5C 052 80 854

As last plus Louis Martinez (bgo).   *LA, March 8, 1949*
                  CHICO'S BOP   Swing Treasury ST 100
                  IT TAKES A WOMAN TO TAKE A MAN —
                  VOC TERRY SWOPE
                  TREES   ,,
                  AFTER YOU'VE GONE (SEPTET: Mettome, Goodman, Gray, Greco,
                     Beecher, Lombardi, Igoe)   Swing Treasury ST 100
                  UNDERCURRENT BLUES   ,,

LA, March 11, 1949 b'cast
                  SWEET GEORGIA BROWN (SEPTET)   Swing Treasury ST 100

LA, March 22, 1949 b'cast
                  BLUE LOU   Swing Treasury ST 100

LA, March 25, 1949
                  JERSEY BOUNCE   Swing Treasury ST 100
                  KING PORTER STOMP   Swing Treasury ST 100

LA, March 30, 1949
                  EL GRECO   Swing Treasury ST 100

Billy Byers (tb) repl. Bernhart. Martinez out.   *LA, March 31, 1949*
4127   THE HUCKLE-BUCK — VOC THE SINGERS Capitol 5C 052 80 854

LA, April 14, 1949
4203   BEDLAM (SEPTET)   Capitol 5C 052 80 854
4206   BLUE LOU   ,,

117

BENNY GOODMAN AND HIS ORCHESTRA

Doug Mettome, John Wilson, Ziggy Schatz, Al Stewart (t), Mario Dione, Billy Byers, George Monte (tb), Benny Goodman (cl), Mitch Goldberg, Angelo Cicalese (as), Wardell Gray, Eddie Wasserman (ts), Joe Casalaro (bars), Buddy Greco (p), Francis Beecher (g), Bob Carter (b), Sonny Igoe (d).

NYC, October 15, 1949

| 4288 | EGG HEAD | Capitol 5C 052 80 854 |

BENNY GOODMAN TRIO

Benny Goodman (cl), Teddy Wilson (p), Gene Krupa (d). *NYC, April 1 1951*
(The Fletcher Henderson Fund b'cast)

		Tax m 8041
	CHINA BOY	
	BODY AND SOUL	"
	RUNNIN' WILD	"
Add Eddie Safranski (b)		
	ON THE SUNNY SIDE OF THE STREET	"
Add Johnny Smith (g)		
	AFTER YOU'VE GONE	"
Add Lou McGarity (tb)		
	BASIN STREET BLUES	"
Trio only:		
	ROSE ROOM	"
Add Buck Clayton (t), Smith, Safranski		
	HONEYSUCKLE ROSE	"
Trio only:		
	I FOUND A NEW BABY	"
Add Clayton, McGarity, Smith, Safranski		
	ONE O'CLOCK JUMP	"

BENNY GOODMAN WITH STRINGS

Hal Diner, Bill Schaefer, Al Thompson (t), Benny Goodman (cl), Eudice Shapiro, Samuel Cytron, Mischa Russell, Felix Slatkin, Paul Nero, Sam Middleman, Harry Bluestone, Robert Suchel, Ted Rosen (v), Virginia Majewski, David Sterkin (viola), Cy Bernard, Victor Gottlieb (co), Paul Smith (p), George Van Eps (g), Morty Corb (b), Nick Fatool (d). *LA, March 5, 1952*

| RHCO 10140 | EMBRACEABLE YOU | CBS 21064 |

BENNY GOODMAN QUINTET/SEXTET

Charlie Shavers (t), Benny Goodman (cl), Mel Powell (p), George Duvivier (b), Jo Jones (d). *NYC, November 8, 1954*

| 20527 | AIR MAIL SPECIAL | Capitol ED 2604261 |

add Steve Jordan (g) *same session*

| 20528 | GET HAPPY | " |

118

BENNY GOODMAN AND HIS ORCHESTRA

Chris Griffin, Ruby Braff, Bernie Privin, Carl Poole (t), Will Bradley, Cutty Cutshall, Vernon Brown (tb), Benny Goodman (cl), Hymie Schertzer, Paul Ricci (as), Boomie Richmond, Al Klink (ts), Sol Schlinger (bars), Mel Powell (p), Steve Jordan (g), George Duvivier (b), Bobby Donaldson (d).   *NYC, November 9, 1954*

20531	JERSEY BOUNCE	Capitol ED 2604261
20532	WHEN I GROW TOO OLD TO DREAM	,,
20533	YOU BROUGHT A NEW KIND OF LOVE TO ME	,,
20534	BLUE LOU	,,
20535	JUMPIN' AT THE WOODSIDE	,,
20536	STOMPIN' AT THE SAVOY	,,
20537	SENT FOR YOU YESTERDAY HERE YOU COME TODAY	,,

Goodman, Powell, Donaldson only.   *NYC, November 16, 1954*

20548	WHAT CAN I SAY AFTER I SAY I'M SORRY	,,

add Braff, Duvivier. *same session*

20549	ROCK RIMMON	,,
20550	YOU'RE A SWEETHEART	,,

Full band as November.   *NYC, November 17, 1954*

20553	BIG JOHN'S SPECIAL	,,
20554	LET'S DANCE	,,

BENNY GOODMAN

Ruby Braff (cnt), Urbie Green (tb), Benny Goodman (cl), Paul Quinichette (ts), Teddy Wilson (p), Perry Lopez (g), Milt Hinton (b), Bobby Donaldson (d).
     NYC, March 25/26, 1955

RL 7673-1	DON'T BE THAT WAY	Philips 6379 001
	ROSE ROOM	,,
	BETWEEN THE DEVIL AND THE DEEP BLUE SEA	,,
	BODY AND SOUL (BG and rhythm only)	Philips 6379 001, 6321 114
	AFTER YOU'VE GONE (BG and rhythm only)	,,
RL 7673-2	SLIPPED DISC	,,
	ON THE ALAMO	Philips 6379 001
	JUST ONE OF THOSE THINGS	
	(BG and rhythm only)	Philips 6379 001, Philips 6321 114
	BLUE AND SENTIMENTAL	
	(PQ and rhythm only)	Philips 6379 001
	AIRMAIL SPECIAL	,,
RL 7673-3	I FOUND A NEW BABY	
	(BG and rhythm only)	Phillips 6370 002, Philips 6321 114
	AS LONG AS I LIVE	Philips 6379 002
	FLYING HOME	,,
	'DEED I DO	,,
RL 7673-4	AVALON	,,

	MEMORIES OF YOU	Philips 6379 002, Philips 6321 114
	STOMPIN' AT THE SAVOY	Philips 6379 002
	IF I HAD YOU	"
	SING, SING, SING	"
RL 7673-5	OH! LADY BE GOOD. (BG and rhythm only)	Philips 6379 003, Philips 6321 114
	STAIRWAY TO THE STARS (UG and rhythm only)	Philips 6379 003
	HONEYSUCKLE ROSE	"
	NICE WORK IF YOU CAN GET IT (BG and rhythm only)	"
	ROSETTA	Philips 6379 003, Philips 6321 114
RL 7673-6	MEAN TO ME	Philips 6379 003
	SHINE	Philips 6379 003, Philips 6321 114
	NIGHT AND DAY	Philips 6379 003
	ONE O'CLOCK JUMP	"
	GOOD-BYE	"

BENNY GOODMAN AND HIS ORCHESTRA

Buck Clayton, Chris Griffin, John Best, Conrad Gozzo, Irving Goodman (t), Murray McEachern, Urbie Green, Jimmy Priddy (tb), Benny Goodman (cl), Hymie Schertzer, Blake Reynolds (as), Babe Russin, Stan Getz (ts), Teddy Wilson (p), Allen Reuss (g), George Duvivier (b), Gene Krupa (d), Martha Tilton (vcl). Trio: Goodman, Wilson, Krupa.
Quartet: Goodman, Lionel Hampton (vib), Wilson, Krupa.
Octet: Clayton, Green, Goodman, Getz, Wilson, Reuss, Divivier, Krupa.
Add Harry James (t) to full band personnel (–1), and add Mannie Klein (t) (–2)

LA, August, 1955 (for soundtrack of *The Benny Goodman Story*)

89016	LET'S DANCE	Coral COPS 5162 D/1-2
89017	DOWN SOUTH CAMP MEETING	"
89018	KING PORTER STOMP	"
89019	IT'S BEEN SO LONG	"
89020	ROLL'EM	"
89021	BUGLE CALL RAG	"
89022	DON'T BE THAT WAY	"
89023	YOU TURNED THE TABLES ON ME – VOC MT	"
89024	GOODY GOODY	"
89025	SLIPPED DISC (OCTET)	"
89026	STOMPIN' AT THE SAVOY	"
89027	ONE O'CLOCK JUMP	"
89028	MEMORIES OF YOU (TRIO)	"
89029	CHINA BOY (TRIO)	"
89030	MOONGLOW (QUARTET)	"

120

89031	AVALON (QUARTET)	"
89032	AND THE ANGELS SING – VOC MT (–2)	"
89033	JERSEY BOUNCE	"
89034	SOMETIMES I'M HAPPY	"
89035	SHINE (–1)	"
89036	SING, SING, SING (–1)	"

BENNY GOODMAN QUINTET

Benny Goodman (cl), Roland Hanna (p), Billy Bauer (g), Arvell Shaw (b), Roy Burnes (d),   *Brussels, May 1958*

THE MAN I LOVE/OH! LADY BE GOOD./
SOMEBODY LOVES ME/I GOT RHYTHM   CBS 21064

Benny Goodman (cl), Russ Freeman (p-1), André Previn (p-2), Barney Kessel (g), Leroy Vinnegar (b), Frank Capp (d).   *LA, September 8, 1958 TV show*
POOR BUTTERFLY (–1)   Festival 246, Rarities 30
AVALON (–1)   "
IT'S ALL RIGHT WITH ME (–2)   "

Benny Goodman (cl) with unk.rhythm section.   *NYC, January 6, 1959 TV show*
WHISPERING   Festival 246, Rarities 30

BENNY GOODMAN OCTET

Urbie Green (tb), Benny Goodman (cl), Zoot Sims (ts), Russ Freeman (p), Don Lamond (d) plus unk. t, g, b.   *Same TV show*
DIGGA DIGGA DO   Festival 245, Rarities 30

BENNY GOODMAN AND HIS ORCHESTRA

Jack Sheldon (t), Bill Harris (tb), Benny Goodman (cl), Jerry Dodgion (as,fl), Flip Phillips (ts), Red Norvo (vib), Russ Freeman (p), Jimmy Wyble (g), Red Wootten (b), John Markham (d), Anita O'Day (vcl).   *Berlin (poss.other locations too)*
October 22, 1959 b'cast (poss. other dates too)
GO, MARGOT, GO   Swing House SWH 24
GET HAPPY   "
RAISING THE RIFF   "
BILLIE'S BOUNCE (p, b, d only)   "
TEN-BONE   "
HONEYSUCKLE ROSE – VOC AO'D   "
SLIPPED DISC   "
BREAKFAST FEUD   "

BENNY GOODMAN QUARTET

Benny Goodman (cl), Lionel Hampton (vib), Jess Stacy (p), Gene Krupa (d).   *NYC, December 17, 1959 TV show*
AVALON   Festival 246, Rarities 30
WHERE OR WHEN   "
I GOT RHYTHM   "

121

Benny Goodman (cl), Jess Stacy (p), Rolly Bundock (b), Jack Sperling (d), Dinah
Shore (vcl).   *NYC, February 28, 1960 TV show*

THESE FOOLISH THINGS — VOC DA	Festival 246, Rarities 30
THAT'S A PLENTY	"
SLIPPED DISC	"
AFTER YOU'VE GONE	"

BENNY GOODMAN AND HIS ORCHESTRA
Jack Sheldon (t), Murray McEachern (tb), Benny Goodman (cl), Jerry Dodgion
(as), Flip Phillips (ts), Red Norvo (vib), Russ Freeman (p), Red Wootten (b), John
Markham(d), Maria Marshall (vcl).   *NYC, September 30, 1960 TV show*

SEPTEMBER SONG	
(cl,vib,p,b,d only)	Festival 246, Rarities 21
THE WORLD IS WAITING FOR THE SUNRISE	
(add g)	"
BILL BAILEY WON'T YOU PLEASE COME HOME	
(as last) — VOC MM	"
I WANT TO BE HAPPY	"

BENNY GOODMAN QUINTET
Benny Goodman (cl), Dave Grusin (p), Karl Kiffe (d), unk. vib, b.
                                          Chicago, mid-October, 1960 TV show

RUNNIN' WILD	Festival 246, Rarities 21

BENNY GOODMAN TRIO
Benny Goodman (cl), Teddy Wilson (p), Gene Krupa (d).
                                          NYC, October, 27, 1961 TV show

AVALON	Festival 246, Rarities 30
BODY AND SOUL	"
CHINA BOY	"
POOR BUTTERFLY	"
I CAN'T GIVE YOU ANYTHING BUT LOVE	"
SHEIK OF ARABY	"

BENNY GOODMAN AND HIS ORCHESTRA
Clark Terry, Doc Severinson, John Frosk, Jimmy Maxwell (t), Bob Alexander,
Jimmy Knepper, Willie Dennis (tb), Benny Goodman (cl), Phil Woods, Jerry
Dodgion (as), Zoot Sims, Tommy Newsom (ts), Gene Allen (bars), John Bunch
(p), Turk Van Lake (g), Bill Crow (b), Mel Lewis (d).
                                          NYC, April 25/26, 1962 TV show

MISSION TO MOSCOW	Festival 246, Rarities 21
CLARINET A LA KING	"
KING PORTER STOMP	"

BENNY GOODMAN QUARTET
Benny Goodman (cl), Lionel Hampton (vib), Teddy Wilson (p), Gene Krupa
(d).   *NYC, February 13, 1963*

WHO CARES?	RCA NL 89304
DEAREST	"

BENNY GOODMAN

Bobby Hackett (t), Rex Peer (tb), Benny Goodman (cl), Modesto Bresano (ts), John Bunch (p), Jimmy Rowser (b), Ray Mosca (d).

Washington, D.C., July 9, 1963
TV show

	THERE'LL BE SOME CHANGES MADE	Festival 246, Rarities 30
	I'VE FOUND A NEW BABY	"

BENNY GOODMAN QUARTET

As February 13, 1963.   *NYC, August 26, 1963*

P4RM 6064	SEVEN COME ELEVEN	RCA NL 89304
P4RM 6065	SAY IT ISN'T SO	"
P4RM 6066	I'VE FOUND A NEW BABY	"
P4RM 6067	SOMEBODY LOVES ME	"
P4RM 6068	RUNNIN' WILD	"
P4RM 6069	I'LL GET BY	"

Same.   *NYC, August 27, 1963*

P4RM 6072	I GOT IT BAD AND THAT AIN'T GOOD	RCA NL 89304
P4RM 6073	FOUR ONCE MORE	"

BENNY GOODMAN QUINTET/QUARTET

Benny Goodman (cl), Lou Levy (p), Al Hendrickson (g), Max Bennett (b), Colin Bailey (d).   *LA, September 17, 1965 TV show*

	POOR BUTTERFLY	Festival 246, Rarities 21
	THE WORLD IS WAITING FOR THE SUNRISE	
	(Hendrickson out)	"

BENNY GOODMAN AND HIS ORCHESTRA

Snooky Young, Yank Lawson, Joe Newman, Dick Perry (t), Chauncey Welsch, Wayne Andre, Sonny Russo (tb), Benny Goodman (cl), Hymie Schertzer, Romeo Penque (as), Al Klink, Tommy Newsom (ts), Don Ashworth (bars), Hank Jones (p), Gene Bertoncini (g), Bob Haggart (b), Bobby Rosengarden (d).

NYC, October 24, 1965 TV show

	LET'S DANCE	Festival 246, Rarities 21
	I WALK WITH YOU (A WALK	
	IN THE BLACK FOREST)	"
	KING PORTER STOMP	"

Goodman, Jones, Bertoncini, Haggart, Rosengarden plus strings from the Don Voorhees Orchestra.   *Same session*

	YESTERDAY	"

BENNY GOODMAN QUINTET

Benny Goodman (cl), Dick Hyman (p), Charlie Byrd (g), Bob Haggart (b), Ed Shaughnessy (d).   *NYC, March 25, 1966. TV show*

	GREAT DAY	Festival 246, Rarities 21
	THE SHADOW OF YOUR SMILE	"
	AIR MAIL SPECIAL	"

BENNY GOODMAN

Benny Goodman (cl) with studio orchestra directed by Milton Delugg.

NYC, June 20, 1967. TV show

A STRING OF PEARLS — Festival 246, Rarities 21

BENNY GOODMAN AND HIS ORCHESTRA

Kenny Baker, Bert Ezzard, Tommy McQuator, Derek Healey (t), Laddie Busby, Johnny Marshall, Jackie Armstrong, Chris Smith (tb), Benny Goodman (cl), Bob Burns, Roy Willox (as), Tommy Whittle, Frank Reidy (ts), Don Honeywill (bars), Bill McGuffie (p), Judd Proctor (g), Lennie Bush (b), Ronnie Stephenson (d). *London, October 28 and November 27, 1969*

THIS GUY'S IN LOVE WITH YOU	Philips 630 8023
YESTERDAY	"
THAT MY LOVE	"
I WILL WAIT FOR YOU	"
LIZA	"
ON A CLEAR DAY	"
AFTER I SAY I'M SORRY	"
I TALK TO THE TREES	"

Kenny Baker (t), George Chisholm (tb), Benny Goodman (cl), Tommy Whittle (ts), Bill McGuffie (p), Judd Proctor (g), Lennie Bush (b), Ronnie Stephenson (d). *London, November 28, 1969*

EASY TO REMEMBER	Philips 630 8023
OCTOPUS'S GARDEN	"
YOU TOOK ADVANTAGE OF ME	"

Derek Watkins, Greg Bowen, John McLeavy (t), Nat Peck, Keith Christie, Jimmy Wilson (tb), Benny Goodman (cl), Bob Burns, Don Honeywill (as), Bob Efford, Frank Reidy (ts), Dave Willis (bars), Bill McGuffie (p), Louis Stewart, Bucky Pizzarelli (g), Lennie Bush (b), Bobby Orr (d). *Stockholm, February 20, 1970*

LET'S DANCE	Decca DDS 3
SWEET GEORGIA BROWN	"
IF I HAD YOU	"
BAUBLES, BANGLES AND BEADS	"
STEALIN' APPLES	"
I WOULD DO MOST ANYTHING FOR YOU	"
TURKISH MARCH	"
SING, SING, SING	Decca DDS 3, Teledec 6.24014
GOOD-BYE	Decca DDS 3
DON'T BE THAT WAY	Decca DDS 3, Teledec 6.24014
WILLOW WEEP FOR ME	Decca DDS 3
BIG JOHN SPECIAL	"
BODY AND SOUL	"
A STRING OF PEARLS	Decca DDS 3, Teledec 6.24014
POOR BUTTERFLY	Decca DDS 3

DEAR DAVE	„
ROLL'EM	Decca DDS 3, Teledec 6.24014
BLUE SKIES	Decca DDS 3
ONE O'CLOCK JUMP	Decca DDS 3, Teledec 6.24014

BENNY GOODMAN ALL STAR SEXTET

Benny Goodman (cl), Zoot Sims (ts), Pete Appleyard (vib), Bill McGuffie (p), Bucky Pizzarelli (g), Harold Gaylor (b), Mousey Alexander (d).   *Copenhagen, 1972*

I WANT TO BE HAPPY	Decca DKL 4/1,2
A SMO-O-O-OTH ONE	„
JITTERBUG WALTZ	„
WHERE OR WHEN	„
HONEYSUCKLE ROSE	Decca DKL 4/1,2 Teledec 6.24014
MY FUNNY VALENTINE	Decca DKL 4/1,2
OH! LADY BE GOOD	Decca DKL 4/1,2, Teledec 6.24014
ROSE ROOM	Decca DKL 4/1,2
MEDLEY: SOON/SOMEBODY LOVES ME/	
FASCINATIN' RHYTHM	„
I'VE FOUND A NEW BABY	„
MEMORIES OF YOU	„
FLYING HOME	„
MEDLEY: DON'T BE THAT WAY/	
STOMPIN' AT THE SAVOY	Decca DKL 4/1,2, Teledec 6.24014
THE SHEIK OF ARABY	„
IT HAD TO BE YOU	Decca DDS 3
TOO CLOSE FOR COMFORT	„
AFTER YOU'VE GONE	„
MOONGLOW	„
RUNNIN' WILD	„
GOOD-BYE	„

BENNY GOODMAN

Benny Goodman (cl), Hank Jones (p), Bucky Pizzarelli (g), Milt Hinton (b), Grady Tate (d).   *NYC, September 15, 1975*

ALONE TOGETHER	CBS 25157
SEND IN THE CLOWNS	„
AND THE ANGELS SING	„
I ONLY HAVE EYES FOR YOU	„

Al Grey (tb), Benny Goodman (cl), John Bunch (p), Bucky Pizzarelli, George Benson (g), Ron Carter (b), Grady Tate (d).   *NYC, September 23, 1975*

I COVER THE WATERFRONT	CBS 25157
A SMO-O-O-OTH ONE	„
YOU ARE THE SUNSHINE OF MY LIFE	„
SEVEN COME ELEVEN	„

Benson out. *Same session*

SWEET LORRAINE	CBS 25157

Urbie Green (tb), Benny Goodman (cl), Pete Appleyard (vib), Joe Venuti (v), Hank Jones (p), Bucky Pizzarelli (g), Slam Stewart (b), Grady Tate (d).

NYC, November 14, 1975

SLIPPED DISC	CBS 25157
LIMEHOUSE BLUES	"

BENNY GOODMAN AND HIS ORCHESTRA

Jack Sheldon, Warren Vache jr, Victor Paz (t), Wayne Andre, George Masso (tb), Benny Goodman (cl), Sol Schlinger (as), Buddy Tate, Frank Wess (ts), Lionel Hampton (vib), Mary Lou Williams, John Bunch, Jimmy Rowles (p), Cal Collins, Wayne Wright (g), Michael Moore (b), Connie Kay (d), Martha Tilton, Debi Craig (vcl), and others.

NYC, January 16, 1978 Carnegie Hall

LET'S DANCE	Decca DBC 3/4
I'VE FOUND A NEW BABY	"
SEND IN THE CLOWNS	"
LOCH LOMOND — VOC MT	"
STAR DUST	"
I LOVE A PIANO — VOC BG	"
ROLL 'EM	"
KING PORTER STOMP	"
ROCKY RACCOON	"
YESTERDAY	"
THAT'S A PLENTY	"
HOW HIGH THE MOON	"
MOONGLOW	"
OH! LADY BE GOOD	"
JERSEY BOUNCE	"
SEVEN COME ELEVEN	"
SOMEONE TO WATCH OVER ME	"
PLEASE DON'T TALK ABOUT ME WHEN I'M GONE	"
DON'T BE THAT WAY	"
STOMPIN' AT THE SAVOY	"
AND THE ANGELS SING	"
WHY DON'T YOU DO RIGHT	"
A STRING OF PEARLS	"
SING, SING, SING	"
GOOD-BYE	"

BENNY GOODMAN

Jack Sheldon (t), Wayne Andre (tb), Benny Goodman (cl), Buddy Tate (ts), John Bunch (p), Cal Collins (g), Major Holley (b), Connie Kay (d).

LA, June 24, 1978

OH! LADY BE GOOD	Century
HERE'S THAT RAINY DAY	"
MAKIN' WHOOPEE	"
I'VE GOT IT BAD AND THAT AIN'T GOOD	"
AIN'T MISBEHAVIN'	"
ALL OF ME	"

DARN THAT DREAM	"
ALONE TOGETHER	"
LIMEHOUSE BLUES	"

BENNY GOODMAN BAND

Tony Terran (t), Dick Nash (tb), Benny Goodman (cl), Teddy Wilson (p), Eddie Duran (g), Al Obidenski (b), John Markham (d), Rare Silk (vcl).

Tokyo, September 3, 1980

	East World EWJ 80187
AVALON	
BODY AND SOUL	"
OH! LADY BE GOOD	"
THE WORLD IS WAITING FOR THE SUNRISE	"
THAT'S A PLENTY	"
BROADWAY – VOC RS	"
GOODY GOODY – VOC RS	"
DON'T BE THAT WAY/	
STOMPIN' AT THE SAVOY	"
MEMORIES OF YOU	"

Osaka, September 6, 1980

AIR MAIL SPECIAL – VOC RS	"
SWEET GEORGIA BROWN	"

Yokohama, September 7, 1980

SING, SING, SING – VOC RS	"
GOOD-BYE	"

Some examples of Benny Goodman's classical performances can be found on the following albums:

Benny Goodman with the Chicago Symphony Orchestra, cond. Jean Martinon: Weber's Clarinet Concerto No 1 in F minor, Op 73 and Clarinet Concerto No 2 in E flat, Op 74   RCA SAR 22043/RCA Victrola VICS 2003

Benny Goodman with the Boston Symphony Orchestra, cond. Charles Munch: Mozart's Clarinet Concerto K626 and Benny Goodman with the Boston Symphony String Quartet: Mozart's Clarinet Quintet K581

RCA Victrola VL 89576

Benny Goodman has also recorded Stravinsky's Ebony Concerto (written originally for Woody Herman). This is available on CBS MP 39768. This album contains other quasi-jazz music performed by, among others, Dave Brubeck and Leonard Bernstein.

BENNY GOODMAN ON FILM

The music of Benny Goodman has been used on numerous soundtracks – not least for *The Benny Goodman Story* – but, as indicated in the main text, Benny made a number of personal appearances in movies over the years. Anyone wishing to see a full list of his on-screen and soundtrack work is directed to David Meeker's comprehensive book, *Jazz in the Movies*.

The following is a short list of Benny's main screen appearances together with, where appropriate, a note of soundtrack recordings which are available (but hard to find).

Adventures in Sharps and Flats (1963) 22 mins. Promotional film by the Selmer Company.

Ben Pollack and his Park Central Orchestra (1929) 9 mins. Vitaphone short of Pollack's band which includes Benny, Jack Teagarden, Jimmy McPartland. (An excerpt from this film was used in a 1962 TV film, *Ben Pollack and his Pick-A-Rib Boys*).

The Big Broadcast of 1937 (1936) 99 mins. Variety show format movie featuring many showbiz stars of the day. An excerpt from this film is used in *Feather on Jazz* (1967), a series of 13 × 10 mins TV shows. Benny and the band's performance of *Bugle Call Rag* from the soundtrack is on Extreme Rarities LP 1002.

The Gang's All Here (1943) 104 mins. A feature film featuring Benny and his band. This movie is sometimes titled: *The Girls He Left Behind* or *Banana Split*.

Hollywood Hotel (1937) 101 mins. A feature film with Benny and the band and Quartet. Excerpts were used in *Auld Lang Syne* (1937); *Brother, Can You Spare a Dime?* (1975); *Hooray for Hollywood* (1976). A track by the Quartet is on Extreme Rarities LP 1002 and several numbers including *Sing, Sing, Sing* are on the soundtrack album: *Hollywood Hotel* on Hollywood Soundstage HS 5004.

March of Time Volume 10 Issue 12 (1944) 21 mins. Benny lectures at the Juilliard School of Music and plays.

The Powers Girl (1942) 94 mins. Feature film with Benny's band and Peggy Lee. This movie is sometimes titled *Hello! Beautiful*. One track by the Quartet is on Extreme Rarities LP 1004.

A Song Is Born (1948) 112 mins. Feature film with Benny in an acting role but also playing. Benny plays on two tracks included on a Louis Armstrong album on Rare Records LP 6.

Stage Door Canteen (1943) 133 mins. Variety show format with many stars of the day including Benny and the band.

Steve Allen in Movieland (1955) TV show made during shooting of *The Benny Goodman Story*.

Sweet and Lowdown (1944) 76 mins. Feature film with extensive appearances by Benny and the band and Quartet.

Swing Into Spring (1958) TV show featuring Benny and the band and others.

Swing Into Spring (1959) TV show as above.

Syncopation (1942) 88 mins. Feature film with an All Star band including Benny.

The World of Benny Goodman (1963) 58 mins. TV documentary about Benny.